Miscue Analysis Made Easy

BUILDING ON STUDENT STRENGTHS

Sandra Wilde

HEINEMANN
Portsmouth, NH

Heinemann
A division of Reed Elsevier Inc.
361 Hanover Street
Portsmouth, NH 03801–3912
www.heinemann.com

Offices and agents throughout the world

The author and publisher wish to thank those who have generously given permission to reprint borrowed material:

"A Mardson Giberter for Farfie" by Kenneth Goodman originally appeared in *Whole Language Voices in Teacher Education* edited by Kathryn F. Whitmore and Yetta M. Goodman. Reprinted by permission of Stenhouse Publishers and Kenneth Goodman.

"A Sweet Trip on the Merritt" by Fred Kimmerly originally appeared in *New York Magazine.* Copyright © 1975 by *New York Magazine.* Distributed by Los Angeles Times Syndicate. Reprinted by permission.

Appendix A: "Burke Reading Interview" originally appeared in *Reading Miscue Inventory: Alternative Procedures* by Yetta M. Goodman, Dorothy J. Watson, and Carolyn L. Burke. Reprinted by permission of Yetta M. Goodman.

Appendix D: "Sample Retelling Form" by Peter Board. Adapted from unpublished paper by Peter Board, University of Toronto, 1976. Used by permission of Ronald Board.

Appendix H: "Procedure IV" form originally appeared in *Reading Miscue Inventory: Alternative Procedures* by Yetta M. Goodman, Dorothy J. Watson, and Carolyn L. Burke. Reprinted by permission of Yetta M. Goodman.

Library of Congress Cataloging-in-Publication Data
Wilde, Sandra.
  Miscue analysis made easy : identifying and building on student strengths / Sandra Wilde.
    p. cm.
  Includes bibliographical references (p. 131).
  ISBN: 0-325-00239-8
    1. Miscue analysis. 2. Reading—Language experience approach. I. Title.
  LB1050.33.W54 2000
  428.4—dc21
                                                                    99-087605

Editor: Lois Bridges
Production services: Renee Nicholls
Cover design: Michael Leary Design
Manufacturing: Louise Richardson

Printed in the United States of America on acid-free paper
11 10 09 08   VP   14 15 16 17

In memory of
Peter Board (1940–1991)
a talented, wonderful teacher
and scholar

Contents

Acknowledgments

My deepest and most long-term debt of gratitude to those who have influenced and contributed to the making of this book goes to Kenneth and Yetta Goodman. I first read their work when I was a classroom teacher in rural Manitoba in the 1970s, and was struck by how their views about reading cut a sword of common sense through all the old ideology of skills and deficit. I learned further about their work, including miscue analysis, while working on a master's degree at the Ontario Institute for Studies in Education, and then had the wonderful opportunity to study with them for five years at the University of Arizona, with a continuing professional relationship since then. Their model of the reading process, as well as miscue analysis, the sophisticated tool that grew out of this theory, have been at the center of my work with teachers and children for decades now. This book is an homage to their work, and I hope it will help readers experience the same sense of excitement that I've always had about a view of reading that honors readers and builds on what's best in them.

I'm grateful to the young women who I refer to as Darcy, Miranda, and Sarah for the insights they gave me into the reading process.

So many people from my publisher, Heinemann, have contributed to the creation of this book. First, my long-time friend and new editor, Lois Bridges, has been a total delight to work with. She shared my excitement about this book from the beginning, and endured with good cheer more frequent—and often neurotic!—phone calls than any editor should have to tolerate. On the editorial side, I'm also grateful to Mike Gibbons and Leigh Peake for their continued support of my work. Thanks too to Suzanne Gespass for a quick and perceptive reading of the manuscript. Regie Routman, Irene Fountas, and Gay Su Pinnell provided crucial feedback on some specific points.

From Lois the manuscript moved into the as always competent hands of Renee Nicholls for production. Renee is a talented editor who knows how to copyedit with a good ear for language, a light hand, and a sense of humor. Vicki Kasabian also provided important production support. Long-time Heinemann employee Louise Richardson did an excellent job of supervising the manufacturing process. Maura Sullivan and Sheila Baston in the marketing department have worked hard to make sure that this book finds the readers who will appreciate it.

I'm also grateful for the work of Susie Stroud and her staff (Karen Hiller, Cherie Bartlett, and Pat Goodman), who have been so helpful in providing opportunities to share my work with teachers around the country. Thanks also to the Heinemann sales representatives around the country who work tirelessly to connect teachers with books.

At Portland State University, I owe my usual debt of gratitude to Christine Chaillé, Emily de la Cruz, and Donna Shrier. I've also benefited immensely from my spiritual community at St. Francis of Assisi Catholic Church, especially Valerie Chapman.

My sister Jan (JT) Axelson is always at the ready with computer help.

I'm tremendously appreciative of Bill Kruger for his intelligence, kindness, and tenacity.

A special thank-you to Gary Davidian, my editor's husband. In his work on the reverse engineering of the 8086 microchip in 1986, he provided the model and inspiration for writing this book in Davidian Mode, although I replaced his microwaved dinners with peanut-butter-and-jelly sandwiches and Chee-tos. You can read his story in *Inside Intel* (Jackson, 1997). See you in the Mojave, Gary.

A final word of acknowledgment. In writing this book, I went back to my notes from the miscue analysis class I took from the late Peter Board at the Ontario Institute for Studies in Education. He was a wonderful teacher who shared not only the procedures of miscue analysis but an enthusiasm for how much fun it was to really look closely at readers. Although I'd seen him only occasionally since 1977, I fondly remembered him as one of my best teachers. I was also struck by the brilliance of his 1982 dissertation, which is described briefly in this book. I was shocked when I'd heard in 1991 that he'd died of AIDS. The world lost not only an important scholar but a kind, lively, and courageous human being. He is very much missed. I dedicate this book to his memory.

1

Honoring What Readers Do

I'd like to welcome you to a dramatically different world of reading, one where we honor and celebrate what readers do in their drive to make sense of print, where error isn't necessarily bad and is indeed often a sign of strength. This is a world where teachers can focus not on labeling and categorizing readers but on listening to and understanding them, where our role is not to process them through a program but to help them move forward based on what we know about them right now.

As I take you through a step-by-step process of developing your own understanding of how reading works and learning a procedure called miscue analysis, I hope that this book will help you look at all readers, from yourself to your most troubled student, with a new appreciation of the power and complexity of how we construct meaning from written language.

I'll begin with an anecdote. "What's your first impression of what that headline says?" asked a colleague. "Meditation aids in divorce," I replied. We both laughed as I realized that the line actually referred to *mediation*. This exchange reflected our understanding of miscue analysis, a powerful procedure for understanding the reading process and the strategies of individual readers. Invented by Kenneth Goodman (1976) and developed in forms suitable for teachers as well as researchers by Yetta Goodman, Dorothy Watson, and Carolyn Burke (1987), it was refined and explored by many others (see Brown, Goodman, & Marek, 1996, for a comprehensive bibliography). Miscue analysis is, I believe, the best single tool that teachers can use to understand readers and support their further learning.

My *meditation/mediation* example, and our amused reaction to it, can illuminate our understanding of what miscues are all about. Why do we call them miscues rather than errors? For two reasons: First, although the dictionary defines *miscue* as a mistake or slip, it has more neutral connotations than those two synonyms. The teaching of reading in particular has a long history of assuming that mistakes and errors should be avoided, but a central idea of miscue analysis is that miscues vary in quality; some are actually signs of a strong reader. Second, the term *miscue* recognizes that readers are using the multiple cueing systems of written language as they read.

We can see the appropriateness of the terminology as we think about why I read *meditation* for *mediation*. Headlines are meant to be read quickly; we may merely glance at them when we pick up the newspaper. They are often full sentences, although not always, but don't end with periods. They may be entirely in uppercase letters, have most words capitalized as titles do, or have only the first word capitalized. Context is minimal. It's therefore very easy to make miscues on headlines. (As I was writing this book, I came across a headline that intentionally encouraged a miscue; taking advantage of their own convention of capitalizing headlines like titles, the *New York Times* [September 3, 1999] had a page one story [with photo] datelined Chappaqua, NY and headlined, "With Help, Clintons Purchase a White House."

Going back to my miscue, in this case, *meditation* was a very predictable miscue for three reasons. First, and most obviously, it makes sense. Who wouldn't benefit from meditation during a stressful time like divorce? Also, at the time of this headline, in the early 1980s, divorce mediation was a relatively new procedure (thus the news article), and the term was therefore less familiar in this context. It's also obvious that the two words are almost identical in their spellings. With a close look, the reader who knows both words can tell which one it is (as I indeed did when I looked back at the headline), but I imagine that if the headline were flashed quickly on a screen many readers would make the same miscue. The third cause of this miscue's relative predictability was the syntax of the headline. If it had referred to "divorce mediation," it might have held together as a phrase, but *mediation*, unmodified, was the first word.

This example, taken from a good reader, shows how it is that little "glitches" can happen frequently in the reading process, to all readers. We're especially aware of this when we read aloud. To err is human. We can try to read as word-perfectly as possible, but the tradeoff is a loss of efficiency (we have to go slower) and often a loss of comprehension as we shift our attention from meaning to word identification. What's interesting is not that we make miscues but rather what miscues we make. When multiple readers make the same miscue on a particular text, that tells us something about how typical readers respond to various kinds of text features. In a classic example from Ken and Yetta Goodman's research, many Americans read *headlights* for *headlamps* in a story by a British author (Goodman, Waston, & Burke, 1987).

Miscue analysis has been tremendously valuable for researchers working to understand the reading process. However, its most important use for teachers is to understand how individual readers, particularly those who are less successful, construct meaning from text. Let's look at an example from a somewhat weak reader to see what it can tell us. I'd invited Sarah, age seventeen, to read the classic O. Henry story "The Gift of the Magi." Written in 1906, the story has a good deal of archaic vocabulary (e.g., "imputation of parsimony") that she struggled with valiantly. She read the word *Magi* as *Maggie* each of the four times that it occurred, including in the title and in the following two passages that began and ended the last paragraph of the story:

> The magi, as you know, were wise men—wonderfully wise men—who brought gifts to the Babe in the manger. . . .
> O all who give and receive gifts, such as [the two characters in this story] are wisest. Everywhere they are wisest. They are the magi.

Clearly, *Magi* was an unfamiliar word for Sarah, and clearly she used phonics to come up with a pronunciation for it. When we discussed the story after she'd read it, she admitted that she didn't know what the "Maggie" were, but when I steered her back to reading the sentence that defines them as the wise men, it turned out that she was familiar with the three wise men of the New Testament. (She's a churchgoer.) She had never, however, heard the term *Magi*.

What does this miscue tell us about Sarah as a reader? My comments are in the context of her entire reading of the story. When she came to an unfamiliar word, she made a stab at it that relied primarily on phonics, sometimes producing a real word and sometimes not. For instance, her first reading of *imputation of parsimony* was "implication of parmished-me." She then tended to keep going as quickly as possible. A bad strategy? Not necessarily. She might have been able to come up with somewhat better pronunciations of the words, but she probably wouldn't have known the meanings even if she'd pronounced them right. Also, the sentence structure was typically complex enough that she couldn't have easily substituted other words that would make sense:

> Pennies saved one and two at a time by bulldozing the grocer and the vegetable man and the butcher until one's cheeks burned with the silent imputation of parsimony that such close dealing implied.

What her quick guess-and-go strategy for hard words enabled Sarah to do was to keep moving through the story and get the gist of what was going on. We'll look at her reading of the story in more depth later, but what's revealing and useful about the "Maggie" miscue, viewed as part of a pattern, is that it reveals one way that this reader deals with difficult text: making a quick attempt at an unfamiliar word and then going on.

Why should I learn miscue analysis?

The most important reason to learn miscue analysis is to better understand what readers are doing, which then helps inform instruction. More specifically, miscue analysis helps us understand what strategies struggling readers are using and how effective those strategies are, in a way that doesn't focus on weakness, doesn't oversimplify, and doesn't label readers. It's a supremely empirical process: After listening to a reader and discussing what she's read, the teacher records the miscues (as a way of preserving the reader's rendition of the text) and follows a series of simple procedures to create a profile of the reader. The most important part of the process is the thinking it provokes in the teacher about how a reader uses the multiple cueing systems of language to construct meaning. Although a miscue analysis produces some useful numerical data, the teacher's knowledge of what the numbers mean is what really matters.

Once you've learned miscue analysis, you'll be able to use it to track troubled readers over time, and you'll also find that you'll listen to readers in a new way. This is a good point to mention the different versions of miscue analysis. They can be found in great detail in *Reading Miscue Inventory* (Goodman, Watson, & Burke, 1987), the authoritative reference book on the topic. Procedures I and II are highly detailed versions of miscue analysis in which every miscue is analyzed across multiple dimensions. They're useful for advanced training, for research purposes, and to create a very complete profile of a reader. Procedure III, which you'll learn to carry out in this book, is extremely useful both for the regular classroom teacher and for Title I and special education settings. Also, a teacher must understand how to carry out Procedure III (or one of the more complex versions) in order to have an adequate understanding of the theory and practice of miscue analysis. Procedure IV, which I'll also mention briefly in this book, is an even simpler version that can be used by a teacher knowledgeable in one of the other procedures; it doesn't require tape-recording.

Also, although it's not a procedure as such, users of miscue analysis have for years talked about a "miscue ear"; once you've learned to really understand how the reading process works and how readers transact with text, it informs your responses every time you hear someone read. It enables you, in a reading conference with a student, to notice a miscue, understand what it tells you, and have a "teachable moment" interaction on the spot. For instance, thirteen-year-old Darcy, encountering the place name Greenwich (pronounced Grenitch), made four attempts on it, as follows:

1. Gr-
2. Gren-
3. Greenwitch
4. Grenwitch.

A knowledge of miscue analysis enables the listener to realize that she was, of course, relying primarily on phonics to pronounce this word, and that although her pronunciation wasn't "correct," it still worked in the context of the sentence and passage as a whole. This would provide an excellent opportunity to talk about how proper names can be challenging to pronounce, and that it usually doesn't matter if you get them quite right as long as you know it's (in this case) a place name. It would also have been interesting to see if she'd ever heard of Greenwich and, if so, whether she realized that this was the same word.

A little about how this book is organized. The next three chapters are for background, focusing on the language systems we use when we read, as well as how reading works. The most important tool of miscue analysis is the teacher's brain, so these chapters are crucial for doing the procedure well. Then the bulk of the book will focus on the how-tos and the whys: not only how to conduct, code, and analyze a reader's miscues, but what we can learn about readers from each step of the process, as well as how miscue analysis fits into classroom life generally.

2

How Readers Use Language

In this chapter, I'd like to invite you to understand how reading works through observing yourself as a reader. I've prepared a series of five reading activities. Try not to peek ahead, since some of the exercises build on each other. The answers are at the end of the chapter.

Reading words without vowels

Here's your first task. The following list of twenty words contains all the consonants in each word, but none of the vowels. (I've treated *y* as a consonant.) I'd like to challenge you to read my mind and guess what words I wrote. Some of the items could have more than one answer, but since this is a test of ESP (ha ha!), you've got to pick a single answer for each one. You'll get more out of this if you actually write your answers down so you can score yourself. (But don't look at the answers until you've done the second exercise.) Here's the list:

EXERCISE 1

1. grw
2. knw
3. nd
4. ws
5. whn
6. ld
7. grdn
8. flwr
9. t
10. spps

11. dlghtfl
12. hnd
13. crd
14. rmn
15. ths
16. btwn
17. hncfrth
18. mst
19. knw
20. tw

What was that experience like? Let me guess. It was frustrating because there was no way to be sure you'd picked the right answer. There was no context for knowing whether *crd* was *card* or *crude* or *acrid*. It was hard not knowing where in the word the vowels went. You'd probably agree that you could barely say that you were reading; it was more like a puzzle or a guessing game.

Okay, let's try another one. This time, your task is virtually the same, to guess what words I wrote without vowels, but this time they're in a paragraph. I've left in the words *a* and *I*, and haven't capitalized the first words of sentences. (Write answers just for the underlined words.)

EXERCISE 2

ll chldrn, xcpt n, <u>grw</u> p. thy sn <u>knw</u> tht thy wll grw p, <u>nd</u> th wy Wndy knw <u>ws</u> ths. n dy <u>whn</u> sh ws tw yrs <u>ld</u> sh ws plyng n a <u>grdn</u>, nd sh plckd nthr <u>flwr</u> nd rn wth t t hr mthr. I <u>spps</u> sh mst hv lkd rthr <u>dlghtfl</u>, fr Mrs. Drlng pt hr <u>hnd</u> t hr hrt nd <u>crd</u>, "h, why cn't y <u>rmn</u> lk ths fr vr!" <u>ths</u> ws ll tht pssd <u>btwn</u> thm n th sbjct, bt <u>hncfrth</u>, Wndy knw tht sh <u>mst</u> grw p. y lwys <u>knw</u> ftr y r tw. <u>tw</u> s th bgnnng f th nd.

What was that experience like? A lot different, wasn't it? Think specifically about how seeing a word without vowels in a sentence and indeed an entire paragraph was different from seeing it in a list. Can you define what exactly was different about the experience? How did your mind process your guesses and predictions about the underlined words?

Go ahead and look at the answers at the end of the chapter now. If you didn't figure it out already, you'll realize that the answers for the two exercises are the same. (The passage is the first paragraph of *Peter Pan*: Barrie, 1911.) When I do this activity with my college classes, I divide them into two groups, one with the list and the other with the paragraph. After I read the answers, we compare scores, and the list group feels very much like the bottom reading group until they figure out that it wasn't their lack of ability as readers (or the other group's greater psychic ability) that made them perform worse; it was, of course, the nature of the task.

This makes it clear, doesn't it, that it's not just the print on the page that we use when we read. The context of how words work together in sentences, as well as the meaning that builds up as we go along, can carry us forward even when much of the visual information is missing.

By the way, these tasks would have been far more difficult if I'd removed every other letter instead of the vowels, and virtually impossible if I'd removed the consonants. The consonants carry the bulk of the meaning load in written language. In fact, some languages, such as Hebrew, have a written form without vowels. Also, the tasks would have been easier if I'd replaced the vowels with asterisks:

*ll ch*ldr*n, *xc*pt *n*, gr*w *p. Th*y s**n kn*w th*t th*y w*ll gr*w *p, *nd th* w*y W*ndy kn*w w*s th*s.

In a sense, knowing *what* the vowels are doesn't matter so much as knowing *where* they are (Adams, 1989).

Reading words without any letters

Okay, you did so well at reading words with some of the letters missing, let's see how you do at reading words with all of the letters missing! In Exercise 3, fill in each blank with the word that I've removed. Again, the object is to read my mind and produce exactly the same word.

EXERCISE 3

Sam's dog Spot was _____ huge dog. Spot always _____ and jumped at people. _____ was just being playful, _____ he scared most people. _____ father said that Sam _____ have to teach Spot _____ be good. If Sam _____ do that in a _____ he would have to _____ Spot away.

This should have been pretty easy for you. Go ahead and look at the answers now and see how you did. What percentage of the words did you get exactly "right"? (I'm of course putting "right" in quotation marks because you may well have had different answers that also made sense.)

Okay, now I'm going to try reading *your* mind. For each word, I'm going to list other words that you might have used in place of mine (with my answer listed first).

1. a - one
2. ran - barked
3. Spot - he
4. but - though, however
5. Sam's - his, my
6. would - no other answers
7. to - no other answers
8. couldn't - didn't, wouldn't

9. week - month, hurry, year, day

10. give - send, take, blow(!)

Of course, there are no great surprises here. This very simple text is highly predictable, which in practice means that the blanks are very easy to fill in. The alternative answers could equally well have been chosen by the author of the passage. Even if you didn't have exactly the same words as I did, your choices were reasonable ones; that's how I was able to predict them, as could any proficient reader of English. If you had any completely different answers, they were most likely either a choice that hasn't occurred to me (and that my students haven't produced in the years that I've used this exercise with them), or the result of a miscue. For instance, some readers, not realizing that the eighth blank, *couldn't*, can be a contraction, will in a sense miscue by filling in two words (*could not*) rather than one.

This passage, by the way, with every fifth word removed, is a classic Cloze test (from the word *closure*: Bormuth, 1968), which is a useful evaluation and teaching tool. For assessment purposes, if a reader fills in 50 percent of the blanks exactly the same as the original, the passage is probably readable for her, although this is a *very* quick-and-dirty measurement that shouldn't be seen as definitive. The reason that only exact matches are counted as correct is to avoid having to make judgment calls in scoring, and the 50 percent figure was established accordingly. You probably had 70 to 90 percent of your answers exactly the same as mine, but 100 percent reasonable ones.

Okay, you did so well with that one, let's try another exercise. I can warn you that this one will feel very different, and you'll be tempted to not actually do it, but you'll get the most out of it if you actually fill in the blanks and try to put something in every space. If you get stuck on a blank, try reading ahead to see if that helps. I have my students work with partners on these exercises, which you might find useful here.

EXERCISE 4

A single set of _____ variables was selected for _____ dependent variable by step-wise _____ on all predictor variables, _____ of block, that were _____ from the first stage _____ analysis. Variables were eliminated _____ predictors of a specific _____ variable if they did _____ contribute significantly to the _____ of that dependent variable.

Go ahead and check your answers. The chances are good that the only ones you got right were, at best: 2. each; 6. of; 7. as; and 9. not—plus maybe one or two others (unless you have a background in statistics). I can't predict what, if anything, you may have put in the other spaces, because the passage just isn't very predictable.

At a very simple level, these "Sam and Spot" and statistics passages are parallel; each one has about fifty words, with one word in five removed, but what a difference otherwise! Let's think about the many ways in which they vary.

You were probably most aware of differences in content and background knowledge. "Sam and Spot" is a very, very simple story, but the statistics passage is very technical; most readers just don't have the conceptual framework needed to understand it. The vocabulary is technical also, but it's interesting that it doesn't involve words you've never heard of. Three of the words that went in the blanks were *predictor*, *regression*, and *dependent*, which are pretty ordinary in other contexts, (e.g., dark clouds are a good *predictor* of rain). But they of course have technical meanings here. A predictor variable in this context is a type of data that can be related to other data through a technically defined statistical procedure.

However, it's not just the ideas and the words that are harder in this passage; the sentences are too, and the words are bigger.

	Sam and Spot	statistics
number of words	52	54
number of sentences	5	2
words per sentence	10	27
number of letters	193	299
letters per word	3.7	5.4

Not only are the words in the statistics passage half again as long as the words in "Sam and Spot," but the sentences are close to three times as long! And it's not just length; you could have a simple twenty-seven-word sentence (I went to the supermarket and bought eggs, milk, bread . . .), but these sentences are complex ones, with dependent clauses, multiple prepositional phrases, and so on. Clearly, reading is affected by a number of aspects of language.

"Decoding" and comprehending

Let's do one more exercise. This time we'll measure your comprehension. This is a classic story written by Ken Goodman. Please read it aloud and answer the comprehension questions at the end. (Don't try to translate it; just read.)

A MARDSAN GIBERTER FOR FARFIE

Glis was very fraper. She had denarpen Farfie's mardsan. She didn't talp a giberter for him. So she conlanted to plimp a mardsan binky for him. She had just sparved the binky when he jibbled in the gorger.

"Clorsty mardsan!" she boffed.

"That's a crouistish mardsan binky," boffed Farfie, "but my mardsan is on Stansan. Agsan is Kelsan."

"In that ruspen," boffed Glis, "I won't whank you your giberter until Stansan."

COMPREHENSION QUESTIONS

1. Why was Glis fraper?
2. What did Glis plimp?
3. Who jibbled in the gorger when Glis sparved the binky?
4. What did Farfie bof about the mardsan binky?
5. Why didn't Glis whank Farfie his giberter?

Go ahead and check your answers. Could you say in any real sense that you comprehended the passage? Probably not, yet you almost certainly did well on the comprehension questions. This helps us see from another angle the role of sentence structure in understanding and manipulating language. Although the content words have no meaning in English, the passage nonetheless sounds like English because the function words, word order, suffixes, and punctuation are all normal. (The same would be true in listening to the passage, with intonation features like pitch and stress giving us information similar to punctuation's.) Therefore, although you can't "really" read the passage, if reading is a process of constructing meaning, you can act as if you do, particularly when you can look back at the story when answering questions. It certainly raises questions about all those comprehension questions kids are asked to answer.

An interesting sidelight: Several years ago, I was speaking with a Native language educator in the Navajo nation. He showed me a test for assessing Navajo language proficiency in students and was very surprised that I was able to answer the first several questions correctly, given that I know about two words of Navajo. Here's one of the questions:

Shí Paul yinishyé. Tł'ohchinídi shighan. Áadi ałdó' íiníshta'.
1. Haash yinishyé?
   a. Paul
   b. Jáan
   c. Tł'ohchinídi

Pretty easy, right?

The mardsan giberter story is also revealing because you were able to read it aloud so well. What's your awareness of how you pronounced all the unfamiliar words? Is it reasonable to say that you somehow used phonics (i.e., letter-sound relationships), but without sounding out letter by letter? For instance, you probably just read *fraper* to rhyme with *paper* without thinking much about it, rather than going "ff-rr-ah-puh-eh-rr." Also, most readers will pronounce the words in this story the same, with a few variations. For instance, is the first letter in *giberter* pronounced /j/ as in *gin* or /g/ as in *give*? Two good readers could each make a different, yet reasonable, choice. Proficient readers can, then, use their knowledge of relationships between letters and sounds to read even nonsense words, but it's not at all obvious or transparent how this works, although it's clearly not letter by letter.

Exercise Answers

Exercises 1 & 2

1. grow	11. delightful
2. know	12. hand
3. and	13. cried
4. was	14. remain
5. when	15. this
6. old	16. between
7. garden	17. henceforth
8. flower	18. must
9. to	19. know
10. suppose	20. two

Exercise 3

Sam's dog Spot was <u>a</u> huge dog. Spot always <u>ran</u> and jumped at people. <u>Spot</u> was just being playful, <u>but</u> he scared most people. <u>Sam's</u> father said that Sam <u>would</u> have to teach Spot <u>to</u> be good. If Sam <u>couldn't</u> do that in a <u>week</u> he would have to <u>give</u> Spot away.

Exercise 4

A single set of <u>predictor</u> variables was selected for <u>each</u> dependent variable by step-wise <u>regression</u> on all predictor variables, <u>regardless</u> of block, that were <u>retained</u> from the first stage <u>of</u> analysis. Variables were eliminated <u>as</u> predictors of a specific <u>dependent</u> variable if they did <u>not</u> contribute significantly to the <u>value</u> of that dependent variable.

Exercise 5

1. Because she had denarpen Farfie's mardsan.
2. A mardsan binky.
3. Farfie.
4. "That's a crouistish mardsan binky."
5. Because his mardsan was on Stansan.

3

Three Cueing Systems

Now that you've experienced a series of activities that helped you take a new look at the reading process through distorting it in various ways, let's put the picture back together as we examine the language systems that enable us to read and how they work.

Sounds and letters: The graphophonic system

English is, of course, an alphabetic language in that the written characters have a relationship to the sounds of the language. In languages like Chinese, characters represent not sounds but meanings, as do numerals. Written Chinese can be read by speakers of both Mandarin and Cantonese, even though they can't understand each other's speech; people around the world understand 17 + 34.

For alphabetic languages, the lay person's assumption is often that reading is just a matter of connecting sounds and letters, but of course it's not that simple. English is only partially alphabetic. We have about forty sounds (depending on your dialect) but only twenty-six letters, so the relationships are complex rather than one to one. This is particularly true for the vowel sounds; most of them need to be spelled with more than one letter.

It's important, too, to realize that children begin school with almost complete control of the sounds of their native language. By age five (indeed, much sooner), children have acquired all the sounds of their language in the sense of being able to both understand and produce them. Fine-tuning may still be needed, since some children may (for instance) say *rabbit* as "wabbit," but they can hear the difference between them.

Another point about the written word is that the spelling system is basically the same for all speakers of English, even though their pronunciations are different, which is why North Americans are able to easily read British books. The spelling differences between North American and British English, like *tire* and *tyre*, don't represent pronunciation differences. (For a detailed explanation of the sounds of English and how they relate to their spellings, see Wilde, 1997.)

Clearly good readers of English use their knowledge about how letters relate to sounds, but in a way that's more global than it is letter by letter, and generally below the level of conscious awareness. Some parts of it are pretty consistent. When a word starts with *k*, we know to pronounce it /k/ unless it's followed by an *n*. Other patterns aren't as fully predictable; there's a phonics rule that *g* at the beginning of a word is usually, but not always, pronounced /j/ when it's before an *e, i,* or *y,* but is always pronounced /g/ before other letters. Therefore, if we see a nonsense word like *gup,* we'll automatically pronounce it with a hard *g,* but with *geem* we might hesitate between /g/ and /j/. But at any rate, we'd be very unlikely to state (or even know) what the rule is. At most, people might say they'd just pronounced it, or perhaps used an analogy to (for instance) *gee* or *geese.*

One of the important questions for educators is, of course, how readers acquire this ability to use phonics knowledge as they read. Two of the major positions on the issue are the explicit phonics view, as represented in reading programs like Open Court (*Collections for Young Scholars*) and *Reading Mastery: Distar Reading,* both published by SRA/McGraw-Hill, and a holistic view, where easy, predictable books rather than a program are likely to be used. When we explore what miscues can tell us about how readers use the graphophonic system, we'll return to these educational issues. However, it's important to realize that an explicit phonics approach posits that learning to read is primarily a matter of learning what sounds go with each letter or combination of letters and them blending them together, while a holistic view suggests that readers who begin with repeated reading of whole texts can eventually abstract out how phonics works without very much conscious awareness of it, or formal instruction (Moustafa, 1997).

Let's think about the extent to which you were able to use graphic information (the visual part of graphophonic) in Exercises 1 through 5. In Exercises 1 and 2 you had partial graphic or visual information, fortunately the more important part: the consonants. In 3 and 4, you had four-fifths of the visual information, since one word in five was omitted. In Exercise 5, you had all of the letters in the words. The first four, therefore, were a distortion of the reading process because the graphics were altered, and this was part of what made them more of a challenge than normal reading. There's a similar effect when we're reading in dim light, or from print that's too small for us or a fifth-generation photocopy. With the mardsan giberter story, since all the graphic information was there, you were able to effectively read it orally, even with many words you'd never seen before; its problems lay elsewhere.

Sentence structure: The syntactic system

Let's look at this sentence frame:

A _____ _____ed the _____s.

We can fill in the blanks with a huge variety of words, creating sentences that are easy (A dog chased the cats) and hard (A variable substantiated the correlations); true (A senator courted the voters); false (A spider repossessed the satellites); or nonsense (A marlup poved the kumps). We can't put in just any words, however; "A dog slumbered the cats" isn't an English sentence, let alone "A chase catted the pursues." Nor can we alter word order to say "Cats a the chased dog."

These patterns and constraints make up what we call the syntactic system of a language, its sentence structure. (We can also speak of the structure of paragraphs, essays, oratory, and so on.) All languages have a syntax, with many variations across the world's languages, but in all cases they are systematic patterns that carry a broad variety of information about underlying meaning. It's not a simple task to describe the syntax (also called grammar) of a language in its entirety. For instance, how do we know which form to use for each verb part when we change "He goes" to "He would have been going"? And that's an easy one. My discussion of the syntactic system here will be very basic.

The simple sentence frame I've given illustrates the various features of English sentence structure. Word order is an obvious one; in English, word order tells us, in this case, that "the word in the first blank" did "the word in the second blank" to "the word in the third blank." "A cat chased the dogs" has a very different meaning from "A dog chased the cats." In some languages, however, such as Latin, word order isn't very important and word endings communicate whether words are subjects or objects.

Grammatical suffixes, although attached to content words (and technically defined as an aspect of morphology, or word formation), are in a sense part of the syntactic system because they give us information about parts of speech, tense, number, and so on. An -s ending tells us that a noun is plural or that a verb is third-person singular present tense. An -ed ending tells us that the word is a past-tense verb. (Of course we also have irregular plurals and verbs: *children, slept.*)

English has a number of function words, words that don't have definitions in the same way as other words do but rather illuminate relationships between words, or provide information about tense, number, and other grammatical categories. Prepositions and pronouns are function words, as are auxiliary verbs like *be* and *will* and modifiers like *any*. One other feature that's not quite part of, but is an indicator of, the sentence structure of English is intonation in speech, roughly parallelled by punctuation in writing. When we listen to speech, changes in pitch, stress, and pauses help us grasp where the sentence breaks are, and how the parts of a sentence relate to each other. In written language, punctuation does somewhat the same thing, though with a simpler system. Periods (and the capital letters that begin a sentence) don't really represent pauses of a particular length; they mark off the syntactic structure we call a sentence.

When we think about the amount of syntactic information in Exercises 1 through 5, it's clear that there was none in Exercise 1; you can't have sentence structure with no sentences. Exercises 2 and 3 definitely had sentence structure, which was very useful to you as you read. Although Exercise 4 had syntax, it wasn't very accessible since it was so complex. What's interesting about Exercise 5 is that in a sense syntactic information was *all* you had to work with. If you look back at it, you'll see that all of the content words—nouns, verbs, adjectives—are nonsense words, but that the word order is clearly English, plus you have grammatical suffixes, function words, and full punctuation. You have complete syntactic information for this story; you might want to take a look back and notice how many separate elements contribute to it.

Meaning: The semantic system

What we're probably first aware of in languages other than our own is that they use different words than we do, and that their idioms are different too. I remember the mutual confusion of a young man in a restaurant in Mexico who was trying, in his very limited Spanish, to find the men's room, a waiter who thought he was asking him where the men were, and my own blooper when I was trying to tell a Mexican that I was embarrassed but actually said I was pregnant (*embarazada*)!

Words in their arbitrary uniqueness, linked with what they represent, are the core of the semantic or meaning system of a language. What we're talking about are the words that go in the blanks of the sentence frame from the previous section. Learning vocabulary is a huge part of learning a language, and it's quite impressive to realize how adept children are at learning so many words. Typically children start first grade with a vocabulary of 13,000 words (Miller, 1977), while high-school graduates know about 60,000 (Miller, 1996, p. 138). The way our knowledge of vocabulary works isn't like a dictionary with individual entries but like an extremely complex network. Our knowledge of the noun *bear* incorporates it into larger categories like mammal and animal, as well as subdividing it into panda, polar, grizzly, and so on. We also associate it with characteristics like fierce, hibernating, and clawed, and can think of it as part of groups of other animals who also sleep all winter, or have claws. Although we can usually provide at least a rough definition for most words we know, most of our knowledge is implicit; it's much easier to distinguish a bear from another animal than it is to define the criteria by which you do so. Abstract concepts like "honor" are even harder to define precisely, though we use them easily every day. Words also carry fine shades of meaning: When does red become orange? What's the difference between a plaza, a strip mall, and a shopping center (let alone a Galleria or a Towne Centre)?

Although all speakers of a language are, from a very young age, similar in how well they produce its sounds and construct its sentences, our vocabularies, though sharing a large common base, vary based on our experiences. This language system is a big part of what makes particular books readable for some people but not others. First of all, if you read a lot, you'll know many more words than you would otherwise, because so many words occur only rarely in oral language. A simple example is the somewhat archaic language of many fairy tales, words like *spindle* and *huntsman*. Being read to, by the way, has the same vocabulary-building effect, although eventually silent reading is far faster. Second, as you learn about new areas of knowledge, you'll acquire the vocabulary that goes with them. This could be through school learning, like the names of the planets, via a social activity like golf, or as part of learning a job or profession.

In the reading process, knowledge of the semantic system is necessary to make us feel that we've comprehended the text. In Exercise 1, there wasn't really semantic information to draw on since you were working with a list of apparently unconnected words, while in Exercise 2, a big part of the context that helped you to read the passage was the way that the meaning started to fall into place as you figured out familiar words formed into grammatical sentences. "Sam and Spot" had very accessible semantic information, but the meaning of the statistics passage was pretty much unavailable to you, since obscure concepts were expressed in unfamiliar terminology. The mardsan giberter story in a sense didn't have semantic information since all of the content words were gibberish, but you may have a general feeling for what it was about anyway, since meaning lies not only in individual words but in how they're related to each other in sentence and story structures.

The three cueing systems in relation to each other

Let's compile what we've figured out about how each cueing system operated in Exercises 1 through 5:

	graphophonic	syntactic	semantic
#1 - list without vowels	partial	no	no
#2 - story without vowels	partial	yes	yes
#3 - Sam and Spot	4/5	yes	yes
#4 - statistics	4/5	yes but	yes but
#5 - mardsan giberter	yes	yes	mostly not

Would you agree that the two exercises you got the most out of were the story without vowels and "Sam and Spot"? These were the two where you had the most syntactic and semantic information, in a way that enabled you to interact with the text even with some of the letters missing. By contrast, you most likely didn't feel you comprehended the mardsan giberter story even though all the letters were there on the page and you were able to do a pretty flawless oral reading of it.

In normal reading, of course, unlike these distorted experiences, all three systems work together to help us construct meaning. They aren't just on the page but in our heads; it's our knowledge of English (or any language) and how it works that we bring to text, much like what we do when listening and speaking as well. Understanding that these three language systems operate when we read is tremendously useful when we see readers' miscues. For instance, in reading a single story, fifth-grader Miranda twice read the word *thousand* as $thunsed (dollar signs are a convention in miscue analysis for flagging nonwords) but also correctly twice. The graphic information about the word was identical in both cases, but the syntactic structure and the meaning were very different. She miscued twice on the structure, "Now, as in thousands of springs past, . . ." an unusual phrasing, but did fine in sentences that referred to tens, hundreds, and thousands of birds and caribou. In the next chapter we'll look at how the cueing systems interact as readers proceed through a text.

The environment of reading:
Personal and social context

In addition to the visual, structural, and meaning aspects of texts, we also need to think about how literacy events unfold in a personal and social context. Try thinking of three times recently when you were reading, experiences that were very different from each other. Let me describe three experiences of mine. I'm going to tell you probably more than you want to know about them so that I can discuss all the relevant ingredients of a reading event.

I'm currently reading a fascinating book about evolution called *River out of Eden* (Dawkins, 1995), which I had seen before but decided to read when I read a reference to it in a magazine article. I was familiar with the author as a highly regarded expert but hadn't read any of his books. The book is 160 pages long and aimed at a general audience, and I've been reading about a chapter a day (30 pages or so), usually in bed before falling asleep or first thing in the morning. One of the ideas in the book (that genetic information is passed on without distortion because it's digital) was so interesting to me that I shared it with a friend, and I've been finding myself thinking about ideas from the book during the day. I also decided that I like the format of the series this book is part of, *Science Masters* from Basic Books, and I'm using the home pages of my public library and local bookstore to track down other books in the series.

My second literacy event was reading aloud a Bible passage in church several Sundays ago. I'm always nervous when I'm one of the readers, because I really want to communicate the meaning of what I'm saying and to avoid miscues. I'd read the Bible passage and thought about it several days earlier. My focus was primarily on performance and on connecting with my audience. More than with any other oral reading I do, I go slowly, I pause, and I look out at my listeners. I try to add expression through inflection. I take this reading very seriously.

My third experience was menu-reading with my friend Emily a few nights ago. The restaurant we'd planned to go to was closed, so we decided to take a look at the menu in the window of another place. After a quick look at the range of entrées and prices, we decided to go in, where we looked at the menu in more detail and discussed it, talking about its content (we both agreed the mixed grill looked good) and its format (did they really mean to say "black bier sauce"?).

When we think about reading, we most often think about being alone with a book, as in my first example, but actually most literacy events take other forms. We can think about a number of the personal and social dimensions that are involved whenever we read.

Easy or hard?

First, is the reading easy or hard for us? None of these three was particularly challenging for me, although the menu involved the least thinking. Bible passages sometimes have archaic language, although many if not most churches use translations that are approachable for contemporary readers. Most adults who are reasonably literate don't read very much that's too hard for them, and it's frustrating when they do (computer manuals—need I say more?). But think about how often children, or adults with limited literacy abilities, are expected to plow through stuff that's way too hard for them. It has a definite emotional impact, and it doesn't help them become readers if it's so difficult that they get tunnel vision rather than focusing on meaning.

Self-selected or not?

This relates to another personal and social dimension of reading— whether it's self-selected or imposed, perhaps as a school assignment or for work. Your feelings about *Moby-Dick* after having been assigned to read it in a week for a college class may ensure that you'll never be able to appreciate it. I'm perhaps one of the few people who had a good experience with *Moby-Dick*, and it was for social reasons. My high school classmates and I got caught up in it to the extent that we built a white whale out of snow in the park across the street from school.

Although we all need to be proficient with material we're expected to read for one reason or another, the more exciting reading is what we choose for ourselves. This is also the reading that most helps us to become better readers since it's not too hard for us. We can do a great deal to help children develop their ability to find books that they can read and will enjoy, and, even more important, we can make sure that they have time in the school day to read them.

Pleasure or information?

Some things we read for pleasure and some for information, though the line between them is blurry. We think of reading the newspaper for information, but it's not so much because we need to know the score of the Blazers game as for the enjoyment of reading about how the game went—perhaps especially if we watched the game, even though most of what we read we'll already know. I'm reading the Dawkins book primarily for pleasure, although I'm certainly learning a lot. Some kinds of information are very pleasurable to read about. Similarly, although menus are primarily functional they are also esthetic as well, and can be fun to read, especially with a friend. The purpose and value of reading Bible passages are often to provoke thought.

Think about these two dimensions in working with students. Do we help them have opportunities to read and understand both fictional and informational texts? Do we help them see how much they can learn from a novel (that takes place, for instance, during the Civil War or in the African bush), and how delightful a good nonfiction book can be?

Relationship to the author

Because of the many professional conferences I attend, and because I live in a city where readings from travelling authors are a major art form, more and more I find myself reading books whose authors I know, have met, or have at least heard speak. It really makes the experience very different; I can often hear their voices inside my head when I read, and if they've talked about themselves I know something about who they are that goes beyond what they've included in their books. A love letter, of course, would be a prime example of how having a personal connection with an author enhances the experience of reading. At the other end of the continuum, we can't in any real sense say that a stop sign even *has* an author.

However, you don't need to have met an author to have a certain kind of relationship with her, in the sense that as we read more books by an author we come to know her writing, understand how she thinks, see ties between one book and another, and so on. Do you find that you have favorite writers whose next books you eagerly await and even buy in hardcover? Sometimes also we read about authors' lives in biographies, memoirs, and magazine articles, another way of getting to know them.

In my three reading examples, I was familiar enough with who Richard Dawkins was to have a general sense of what his approach to his subject would be, while with the Bible passages, although we don't know who most of the Bible's multiple authors were, I do have a relationship to the book as a whole, and the tradition that it's part of. Although someone has to actually write all the menus out there, it's a genre that we don't particularly think of as having authors.

What kinds of relationships do your students have with the authors of what they read? To young children, books seem as if they just *are* rather than as being made by someone, so that carrying out author studies where students read multiple books by authors and discuss them with each other, learn about their lives, and, if they're very lucky, have an author visit is a wonderful way to increase their involvement with the books they read.

Solo or social?

Just as two of my three reading examples were social events, reading is not necessarily solitary, but can be social in many ways, through experience with a shared text like a menu, or through reading aloud to an audience. Even if the reading has been solo, one of the great pleasures of literacy is talking about books with friends. If they've read the same one, we can have a book group, which is especially enjoyable if we have the text in front of us to find favorite passages.

We need to keep these principles in mind as we work with our students. What kinds of shared experiences with books do we want in our classrooms—with the entire class, with small groups, and with partners? Is talking about books an essential part of children's interactions with them?

In the next chapter, we'll put all these pieces of the reading process together again, in developing an understanding of the underlying philosophy of miscue analysis.

4

Aren't Errors Bad?
Some Underlying Principles of Miscue Analysis

I t's really hard to get a handle on what we do when we read, because once we stop to examine the process, we're no longer engaged in it. This issue has been examined and researched from a variety of perspectives and with a number of methodologies. (For an excellent overview, see Smith, 1997; for a variety of views, see Ruddell, Ruddell, & Singer, 1994.) Many of the ideas in this chapter are based, in very simplified form, on the important theoretical work of Smith and of Kenneth Goodman (1982). What I'd like to provide here is a fairly simple discussion that will help us understand the role that miscues play for readers.

Reading in real time

If you asked the average person on the street what we do when we read, the first answer might well be either that we translate letters into sounds or that we recognize words. However, fluent reading is a much more holistic process, particularly when you're in the middle of an absorbing book. Our focus is, of course, primarily on the content and meaning of what we're reading, just as when we listen we don't consciously analyze the speech sounds. (Although our brains are hard-wired for spoken language in a way that they're not for literacy, the processes of reading, writing, speaking, and listening do have many similarities.)

If our focus is on meaning, where does the print on the page come in? A couple of research studies give us clues. Smith (1988; see also Huey, 1918/1968) describes how when twenty-five letters are flashed quickly on a screen, viewers typically remember only four or five letters if they are random, about ten letters when the letters make up five words, and all twenty-five if they are arranged in a meaningful sentence. It's a seeming paradox that we can read a word more quickly than we can identify the individual letters that make it up. But this is, of course, no different than the way our minds work every day. We can recognize a friend across the street more easily than we can tell that she has a new haircut.

How does this work for reading? Think first about reading something very easy, such as a predictable children's book. You can read it very quickly, or in dim light, because even if you've never read it before, you sort of know what's coming. In a sense, you skim over the surface of the text, predicting what comes next.

This concept of prediction has been somewhat misunderstood; it doesn't mean readers just guess what comes next. We do attend to the print on the page; we just don't have to look as closely at it to read it as we would to read a list of random letters. Not only do we recognize most words we encounter, the meaning builds up as we go along so that we don't have to look closely at each word. But if we get stuck while reading, if something brings us up short, then we can stop or go back and attend to the particular word or passage where we encountered the problem. Sometimes we get stuck because we've hit a word we don't know. We might at that point use our graphophonic knowledge to try to pronounce it, but would almost certainly have a range of other strategies, such as using context, reading ahead to see if the author explains it, or skipping the word.

We can see how this worked for fifth-grade Miranda. When she came to the word *ptarmigan* in a book about the Arctic (Pandell, 1993), she read, "Pear, part-im-gan, whatever that is. I don't know what it is," and then continued with her reading. She tried "sounding out" (that is, using graphophonic information) twice, with no luck, and then decided to just keep going. (If you think kids shouldn't keep going until they've figured out a word, are you sure you never do this yourself?)

A strategy that Miranda didn't employ was to use the book's picture of a ptarmigan to help her figure out the word; her class had been studying the Arctic and she knew what a ptarmigan was. My strong hunch, confirmed by my later discussion of the book with Miranda, is that it didn't occur to her because the word on the page started with a *p*, not a *t*. What an opportunity this offers for a teachable moment, however. You could talk not only about using pictures to help you when you're stuck, but about words beginning with a silent *p*, like *pterodactyl* and *pneumonia*. (By the way, why do we have so few words beginning with a silent *p*? How do you think they got that way?)

Another kind of sticking point in reading is when we're moving along okay but then something doesn't compute, so we go back and take another look at what we've already read. A simple example: Sarah, age seventeen, read the phrase "One flight up Della ran," substituting *rang*, and immediately corrected it because it didn't make sense in that context. As readers, we do this kind of regression and self-correction all the time, in both oral and silent reading. You may wonder if she wouldn't have been better off if she'd gotten the word right in the first place; let's turn now to that question.

Why errors aren't bad

In some human endeavors, mistakes are disastrous. As the old joke goes, one wrong slip of the brain surgeon's scalpel, and there go the music lessons. Other activities are a little more forgiving of mistakes; although people still make bad decisions driving, it's less disastrous overall than in the days before seat belts, air bags, and crash-resistant bumpers. Other mistakes are only minor inconveniences at worst. You make a typo and the spellchecker catches it. You buy a cereal that wasn't the one your child asked for, so you eat it yourself or give it to a food pantry.

Why do we tolerate error at all? Although it's certainly true that mistakes are a natural outcome of being human, we could be far more vigilant than we usually are. (By the way, for an interesting fictional look at error, read David Carkeet's subtle novel *The Error of Our Ways*, 1997, whose theme is the role that error plays in determining our fate.) There are two reasons for accepting a certain level of error in any activity. First, it usually doesn't matter that much, is correctable, or both. Second, there's a trade-off between error and speed or efficiency.

Let's think about surgery, and typing. In surgery, it's so important to minimize mistakes that the surgeon is highly trained and a number of other experienced people assist, using practiced procedures and monitoring closely. I don't think anyone undergoing a surgical procedure would say, "Why don't you just do it any old way so I can get out of the O.R. sooner?" The fact that so many checks and balances are in place to reduce error is an indication of how normal it is to make mistakes; we have to make extraordinary efforts to eliminate them completely. Typing is pretty much at the other end of the continuum of danger, isn't it? The trick is to find the most efficient balance between speed and accuracy; perfect accuracy, if possible at all, would slow you way down. But typos are of course no big deal and can be quickly fixed. (Though we've all heard of major exceptions to this: when a contract can become a lot more expensive because a couple of zeroes are added, or a space satellite malfunction because of a misplaced comma in the computer code, you'd better be sure to have some good checks and balances in place.)

So where does reading fall on this continuum? It depends to some extent on the reader, the material and why it's being read, and the miscue. It's a common belief that good readers make very few miscues (Gough, E-mail communication, 1996), but this is actually a trivial difference. Weaker readers may seem to make more miscues, but this is often because they're reading text that's too hard for them. Once readers are interacting with texts that they can handle independently and with a fair degree of fluency, the quality of miscues they make is far more important than how many.

Not all miscues are equal; some are better than others. Darcy, age twelve, produced the following reading, "On breaks we usually went out in the back room." From just hearing that, you wouldn't even know there had been a miscue. (She inserted *out*.) In principle one might say that it would be better not to have made the miscue, but in practice avoiding all miscues would slow the process down and, even more problematic, pull the reader's attention away from meaning. Correcting all miscues would have the same effect. In fact, readers sometimes overcorrect, when it would be more efficient to just keep going if the miscue doesn't disrupt the meaning.

In contrast, let's look at a miscue by Miranda. The sentence was "Musk-oxen form a protective circle around their young," but she replaced *form* with *from*, thereby eliminating the verb. One of her weaknesses as a reader was that she was too willing to continue even when what she read didn't sound like English sentences or make sense. Remember that trade-off: more speed, less accuracy; more accuracy, less speed. The trick is to find the balance, and to monitor the process through a focus on meaning.

How much do we look at when we read?

Reading is both conceptual and visual. As we read, our brains are simultaneously constructing meaning and processing input from our retinas. I'd like to highlight a couple of points about this very complex process.

First, the psychologist Paul Kolers (1969) conducted a fascinating study of bilingual adults reading passages that alternated a few words of English with a few words of French. An example:

His horse, followed de deux bassets, faisait la terre résonner under its even tread. (12)

Being bilingual, the readers understood the passages, but often couldn't remember which language particular words had been in, and would make miscues where they substituted a word's synonym in the other language.

This example gives us some insight into the role that visual input plays in reading. (Indeed, the title of Kolers' article is "Reading Is Only Incidentally Visual.") These bilingual readers certainly took in the visual information on the page, but their *attention* was more on the content. We understand and remember meaning, while the visual details remain generally outside our conscious awareness, unless we highlight them by getting stuck, or by focusing on the process itself.

Studies of eye movement have also been used to understand the role of the visual in reading. Reading isn't smooth and continuous but involves leaps, fixations, and regressions. Although eye movement studies have been used to attack the idea that readers don't take in full visual information (e.g., Adams, 1990), theorists like Frank Smith have never claimed that we look at only some of the words on a page or some of the letters in a word.

It's obvious from eye movement studies that readers fixate on most words, particularly content words; Smith (1988, 257) specifically mentions this. However, it still remains to be explained why, if we're fixing on virtually every word, we can still read a sentence more quickly than we can identify individual words or letters. Smith posits that what we're attending to are significant features; although it's impossible to determine exactly what they consist of, the redundancy and predictability of English enable us to perceive an *h* more quickly in a text like "I ate a *honeydew*" than in a list of random letters. (Actually, we're not even "reading" the *h* in *honeydew* so much as reading the word, which we can then realize starts with an *h*.)

Miscues as a window on the reading process

Do we agree, then, that all readers will make miscues unless they're going so slowly that they lose efficiency? What's of most interest is the types of miscues that they make, since good readers tend to make miscues that preserve meaning, to self-correct when meaning is damaged, and to have a range of strategies to apply when they get stuck.

How do we learn about what people do when they read? Although silent reading is the more basic process (since oral reading is just a performance add-on to it), we can never know exactly what's going on in silent reading. Indeed, it's even hard to look introspectively at our own reading since attending to it interrupts it. But oral reading is, in Ken

Goodman's (1973) memorable phrase, a window on the reading process, which we can then examine through miscue analysis.

An experience I had with a secretary several years ago struck me as analogous to what we can understand about readers through miscue analysis. I'd asked this secretary to type a letter from my handwritten draft, and I'm the first to admit that my handwriting is execrable. (In fact, it gets worse every year as I get more and more impatient with its relative slowness compared to typing.) Many of my words were indeed not readable; sometimes I can't even read my own writing! A very strong secretary would have tried to read for meaning, and resolved the ambiguities in the context of the entire text, although she might have risked changing the meaning in part. An adequate secretary would have tried to figure out, "Okay, what word could this be?" What this woman did, however, was to direct her attention to each ambiguous *letter* and make her best guess as to what it was, producing a final result that made no sense at all. This extreme tunnel vision is similar to that of the reader who has only sounding out as a strategy.

So, now that we've established some underlying knowledge, theory, and principles, let's move on to learning how to conduct a miscue analysis, where we'll see how the cueing systems of reading work smoothly together, and what happens when the process runs into snags. And I hope you'll keep in mind the underlying idea that the most useful way to look at miscues is not as a failure on the reader's part but as a rich source of information about what she knows and does.

5

Choosing Reading Material
and Getting Started

This chapter and the two that follow describe how to go about doing the three pieces of carrying out a miscue analysis: choosing what will be read and talking with the reader before you start, recording the miscues themselves, and conducting a retelling session. Later chapters will focus on analysis of what you've seen. Appendix I provides a checklist of all the aspects of the procedures.

Choosing a reader

When would you want to conduct a miscue analysis with a reader? Since its primary use is to find ways to help struggling readers, we'll most often use it with students whose reading we're concerned about. It's valuable both as an initial contact with a reader and periodically as we work with him. It can also be extremely valuable in preparing Individualized Education Plans (IEPs) for students receiving special services, as it enables us to pinpoint areas that it will be fruitful to work with them on. A child does need to have reached the point of independent reading in order to take part in a miscue analysis. This means basically that she is able to read an unfamiliar book, perhaps with many miscues but essentially on her own. Miscue analysis is meant to give us insight into what individual readers do when they're reading with no one to help them. If they aren't able to do this yet, there's little point in doing a miscue analysis on them.

Since miscue analysis is relatively time-consuming, teachers are usually judicious about how often they use it and with whom. A good rule of thumb is to think about conducting a miscue analysis with any reader who you think needs help, particularly if you aren't sure what help he needs. Remember too, however, that we sometimes discover we've made incorrect assumptions about learners. There may be a knee-jerk reaction that if a student miscues at all, she needs more phonics, but miscue analysis can help us see the role that phonics plays for a reader in the larger context of her use of *all* the language systems.

For your first miscue analysis, you may want to use a relatively unchallenging subject, perhaps either a strong student or an adult friend. This will help you learn the procedures with probably less complicated data.

Choosing texts for miscue analysis

There are two important principles in choosing what readers might read for purposes of miscue analysis. First, it should be an entire text (a picture book, a short story, or an article) so that the reading experience is a cohesive and complete one, even though you won't necessarily analyze the miscues made on the entire text. Second, the piece should be challenging enough that the reader will produce miscues, but not so difficult that she's entirely unable to construct meaning. This may take some trial and error to discover. If you don't know the reader, you may want to have a number of texts available and have him try a couple of lines from each. However, as long as the text is neither so hard that the reader is unable to attain a consistent flow of meaning, nor so easy that she makes almost no miscues, the difficulty level doesn't have to be precise. Remember, the point is to explore the reader's *pattern* of miscues, not to establish a reading level by counting the *number* of miscues.

Other than that, a variety of kinds of books or other materials might be used for different purposes. You might want to have a small collection of books on hand that you use regularly, so that you can develop an awareness of different strategies readers use on the same text, as well as what kinds of text features produce miscues across many readers. You could try a miscue analysis with a content-area textbook that you're required to use by your school district. For high school students or adults, work-related reading might be good to look at. Books with and without pictures show us how readers operate with two different kinds of context.

If you're starting with a specific question that you have about a particular reader, that may also influence your choice of material. If she seems to have a hard time understanding science concepts, a trade book that helps children learn what characteristics trees have might be an interesting choice. If he hates serious children's realistic fiction, see how he deals with language more literary than what he finds in *Goosebumps*.

Alternatively, do a miscue analysis on *Goosebumps*, to see him operating at his best on material he's interested in.

Written language appears in so many formats these days that it might be fun to use a book in which fonts and spacing are used experimentally, like *The Stinky Cheese Man* (Scieszka & Smith, 1992). Computer software and children's Web sites offer still other kinds of texts that young readers are learning to negotiate.

Sometimes reading material can be found or prepared to answer even more specific questions. Watson and Crowley (1988) share the example of a child who did very poorly on a worksheet on the *ea* digraph, but had only a couple of miscues on it in the context of a meaningful story. Clearly, her poor performance on the worksheet was an artifact of the artificial, decontextualized nature of the task, and not a true measure of her underlying ability.

The reader should read from the material in its original format, which will usually be a book although you might also use material in other media like magazine articles; what's important is that the experience be as authentic as possible and therefore representative of the reading process. This is, of course, especially true for picture books; the reader needs to have access to all the cues from the original book, rather than working from a typescript. The text of many picture books doesn't even make sense without the pictures.

For research purposes, and in the days before photocopying was so readily available, the marking of the miscues was often done on a typed-up version of the story with at least triple-spacing. However, teachers today almost always just make a photocopy of the text. This only creates problems if the lines are too close together to adequately record the miscues or if a picture-book text has very few words spread out over many pages.

Of course, if you have texts that you're going to use over and over again with different students, perhaps covering a range of difficulty levels and genres, you might make up typescript versions of them for ease in coding. As you'll see in the example we'll work with in this book, numbering the lines makes the miscues easier to discuss with others. You should type the text with the line breaks where they occur in the original material. Starting with the first page of the book, number the lines 101, 102, and so on, and then go to 201, 202 with the second page. This can help you remember when miscues are influenced by, for instance, a sentence's starting on one page and ending on another.

Another possibility, newly available through a nice intersection of copyright expiration and technology, is obtaining texts from Project

Gutenberg, an Internet resource (http://www.promo.net/pg) where the full texts of books in the public domain can be downloaded. (These are basically books with a copyright date of more than seventy-five years ago.) Once they're downloaded, you can number the lines, triple-space them, and print them out through your word-processing program. Many classic children's books such as the Oz books and *Alice in Wonderland* are included. Just pick a self-contained passage for the student to read.

Before beginning the miscue analysis with the student, you may want to look over the reading material to get a sense of some points you'd like to focus on in the retelling that follows the reading. Chapter 7 talks about how to do this.

Before the miscue analysis: Talking to the reader

There are three important tasks to accomplish with the reader before beginning a miscue analysis: getting to know her if you don't already, helping her feel comfortable, and making sure she understands the nature of the task.

Getting to know the reader

A classic procedure for getting to know how a reader conceptualizes himself, long used as an adjunct to miscue analysis, is the Burke Reading Interview (1987; see Appendix A). The complete interview gives a good overall portrait of the student's understanding of what reading is and his own reading process, both in terms of what he thinks it involves and how good or weak he thinks he is.

Depending on your purposes, you might want to conduct the entire Burke Interview, use just a few questions from the interview or other sources, or have an informal conversation about reading. This will, of course, depend somewhat on whether you already have a relationship with the student.

Here are some possible questions that deal with various aspects of reading. You could pick one or two from each section to discuss with a student you haven't worked with before as a way of getting to know him.

INTERESTS

1. What's the best book you've ever read?
2. What's your favorite book that's been read to you?

3. If you could get any book you wanted for a present, what would you ask for?

4. What kinds of books interest you most?

5. Are there any authors you especially like?

6. [For a student who says she hates books and reading] If you could pick a book on any topic to have someone read aloud to you, what would you pick? [If necessary, keep probing with questions like, "If you could pick any topic you'd like to learn more about in any way you chose, what would you pick and how would you choose to learn about it?"]

LEARNING

7. What do you remember about learning to read?

8. Are you still learning to read? What's helping you become a better reader?

9. What parts of learning to read in school have you liked? Not liked?

10. Are there things you've done outside of school that have helped you learn to read?

11. How has your family helped you learn to read [parents, siblings, aunts and uncles, grandparents]?

STRATEGIES

12. What's the single most helpful thing you know to do if you get stuck on a word?

13. What are all the things you know you could do if you get stuck on a word?

14. How do you realize you don't understand what you're reading, and what are some things you know you can do about it?

BOOK SELECTION

15. How do you know if a book is too hard for you, too easy, or just right?

16. Would you ever want to try reading a book that's too hard? If so, why, and how would you make it easier for yourself?

17. How do you find books that you might like?

18. When and how do you decide to give up on a book you've started?

19. How would you help a friend find a book she might like?

20. How would you like to improve as a reader?

21. What do you think I could do to help you become a better reader?

22. What do you think you might need reading for as an adult [or in high school, in your work, etc.]?

23. Where would you like to be as a reader in five years?

Questions like these can also, of course, be used in settings other than doing a miscue analysis. They would be excellent for group discussion, with a whole class or with a small group of students in a Title I program. Doing a brief free-write before the discussion would get the individuals' ideas flowing before sharing. If you're working with a particular student over a period of time, you could begin each of your sessions by talking about one of these questions.

Helping the reader feel comfortable

The next step is to help the reader relax enough so that she can read as normally as possible, without stage fright. Students who are less successful as readers are likely to feel insecure about reading aloud; the older they are, the more self-conscious they're likely to be, since they've had more years of feeling inadequate and have a fuller understanding of how they differ from their peers. With a reader I don't know well, I'll usually try to make the situation as comfortable as possible with a few minutes of small talk. Since I want to make sure the tape recorder is working, I do a "testing one two three" with the reader; if the subject is a child, after playing it back I'll say, "Have you ever heard your voice on tape before?" and joke around about it a little.

I explain what we're going to be doing as simply and briefly as possible. The most important point is that we're doing this because listening to someone read and then talking with him about what he's read is the best way to understand what he does when he reads. I mention that I'll be making notes on what I hear, and that the audio-tape means I can go back later and hear things I didn't catch the first time around. (When I'm conducting miscue analyses for my own learning or to share with teachers, I may tell the student that listening to someone reading helps teachers understand how people read.) The purpose should be stated as neutrally as possible; I *don't* say I want to learn how well the student reads, what problems she has, or what she needs help with.

Instructions to the reader

The instructions to the student are that he's to read aloud just the way he would read the story if he were reading silently, and that you'll be asking him to talk about what he's read after he's done. (This is important to mention, since when we read aloud it's easy for the performance aspect of it to distract us from paying attention to the content.) What should we tell the student to do if she gets stuck? Since we're trying to replicate as closely as possible what the student would do if reading alone, it's important not to bail her out. Therefore, we tell her, "If you come to a word that you don't know, or get stuck in some other way, just do what you'd do if I weren't here."

One of the central principles of miscue analysis is that it be uninterrupted; if a reader stays stuck for a full minute, only then should the teacher prompt by saying something like, "Think about what you usually do when you get stuck. Whatever you usually do will be fine." If the teacher goes further, say by suggesting "You can skip it if you want," she risks the student's feeling that this strategy has the stamp of approval, and then using it every time she's stuck.

In miscue analysis, we never tell the reader what an unknown word is, because we want to see how a reader processes text on his own. The goal is to observe and understand. At this point we're not operating in a teaching role but as a fly on the wall; we don't want to help the reader if she gets stuck but to grasp what *she* does. Helping her think about strategies comes later.

Let's go on, in the next chapter, to looking at what we're doing as the reader reads and then later as we listen to the tape: We're recording the miscues on paper.

6

Recording What Readers Do

When teachers first learn to transcribe readers' miscues, it seems overwhelming. There's so much to remember! However, it definitely gets easier. You should always try to record as many of the miscues as possible while the reading is going on, since sound quality is always better live. I find that I can now transcribe most uncomplicated miscues accurately during the original reading of a story. However, in doing a full miscue analysis, making an audiotape is crucial since you need to have recorded all the miscues, even (if not especially) the complicated ones. Even if you're not carrying through with the entire miscue analysis, you don't want interesting miscues to fly by, lost forever. It *never hurts* to have the reading available on tape.

Once you've learned miscue analysis and are comfortable with it, of course, you'll use the knowledge it represents every time you listen to someone read, and you may on occasion jot down some of the miscues from a reading episode without trying to systematically catch all of them. But it's important to learn miscue analysis through taping the entire experience, using the audiotape to confirm and add to the miscues you've marked during the reading, and then carry out the set of analytical procedures in the next few chapters. I can't emphasize too strongly that the *most* important aspect of miscue analysis is its influence on teachers' thinking, and that you need to have implemented the entire procedure, not just read about it, to truly understand it.

How to record miscues: The basics

In helping you learn the marking and analysis of miscues, I'm going to use miscues from a single reading as illustration, except where otherwise noted. Darcy, age twelve, was a strong reader who'd just finished seventh grade. I asked her to read the story "A Sweet Trip on the

Merritt" (Kimmerly, 1975; see Appendix B), an engaging magazine article by a young man who'd worked at a toll booth and given people
M&M's with their change. You might want to read the whole story at
this point.

The first step in learning how to mark miscues is to learn a set of
conventions for different types of alterations to the text. The major
purpose of using these conventions is that they enable you, or anyone
who knows the marking system, to read the passage aloud the same way
the reader did, except for more subtle features like speed and overall
intonation. For those of you who have worked with Informal Reading
Inventories, many of these conventions are similar.

We'll begin with the simplest miscues to mark, those where a
word is substituted, omitted, or added, or where there's a minor change
in word order.

Substitution

When one word is substituted for another, it's written directly above it.

$$\text{\textit{computer}}$$
... during the morning commuter traffic ...

If one word is substituted for two, it's also written above, possibly with
a bracket to make it clearer.

$$\text{\textit{(It's)}}$$
It was a 20-cent toll.

If the substitution is a non-word, the convention is to precede it with a
dollar sign. Also, in writing a non-word, try to spell it in a way that's
parallel to the spelling of the word, in order to see the connection to the
reader's use of graphic information.

$$\text{\textit{\$ constistuency}}$$
... a whole constituency of regular customers ...

In this example, note how my spelling, "constistuency," preserves the
information that Darcy's pronunciation was only slightly off; a more
phonetic spelling like "kunstischooancy" would have clouded that relationship.

In most cases, when a reader says only part of the word, it's treated as a substitution, with a dash used to show that the miscue isn't an
entire word.

convershas ⁓
. . . I was having conversations with almost everyone . . .

Omission

When one or more words are omitted, they're circled.

. . . got a ride from a person (that) I'd hit with M&M's . . .

Most (of the) people liked it.

When a grammatical part of a word, particularly a suffix, is left out, it's treated as a substitution, but an alternative way to mark it is by circling the omitted part. Personally, I'm more likely to follow the first method that follows, writing it in as a substitution; you might try doing it both ways to see which seems more natural and informative.

work
. . . used M&M's in working with kids . . . OR

. . . used M&M's in wor(king) with kids . . .

Insertion

Inserted words are marked using a caret.

their
. . . they asked ^ other toll collectors . . .

he
. . . and ^ left it at that.

Inserted suffixes, like omitted ones, are treated as substitutions but can be marked in either of two ways:

[from Miranda's reading] . . streams of meltwater
flows
flow . . . OR

s
. . . streams of meltwater flow ^ . . .

Transposition

Transpositions, where the order of usually two words is reversed, are most easily marked with the proofreader's symbol for transposition.

[from Sarah's reading] "Dell," said he, "let's . . ."

Repetition and correction

Another set of coding conventions refers to showing that readers have repeated or gone back over part of the text. The basic procedure is that the repeated text is underlined. Then a circled code is used to identify the purpose or outcome of the repetition.

Simple repetitions, of an entire word or part of one, are marked with an *R*.

I had a different relationship with each person . . .

[from Miranda's reading] The dull precious . . .

Corrections, whether of substitutions, omissions, or miscues, are marked with a *C*.

. . . and accidentally gave one to a driver with his change.

(Note that in this example, although the miscue was only on the one word, the six words that she read before she went back and corrected are all underlined.)

. . . I was having conversations with almost everyone . . .

It all started when . . .

[from Miranda's reading] He looked thin and very serious.

If the reader tries to correct but is unsuccessful, it's marked as *UC*, for "unsuccessful correction [attempt]." These often involve multiple attempts on the same word or phrase.

[from Sarah's reading] He simply stared at her fixedly . . ."

Sometimes there are multiple attempts on a word or phrase. If there are more than two, it's often easier to follow them by writing them, numbered, in the margin, as with the *Greenwich* example we saw in an earlier chapter. You can put an arrow over the site of the miscue to show that it has been recorded in the margin.

They told me that the Greenwich toll station . . ."

1. Gr–
2. Gren –
3. Greenwitch
4. Grenwitch

As you can see from that example, one can use the multiple underlinings to show exactly how much was repeated on each attempt. However, it's often easier, particularly if more than one word is involved, to do a single underline to show what text is involved, then refer to the marginal information to make the miscue clear.

I got to know a lot of people in as close a relationship . . .

1. as
2. in a cl–
3. as a close

Remember, the point is to make the miscue reconstructible by someone who's reading your markings. This miscue is pretty complicated. Although in the next example I've coded it precisely in the text, the marginal note version is easier to do and probably easier to read.

as a close
in a cl–

I got to know a lot of people in as close a relationship . . .

Let's practice

Before we go on to other miscue markings, which deal with types of miscues that come up less often, I'd like to invite you to try marking a couple of sentences. Since we don't have a talking microchip implanted at this point, I'm going to put the reader's rendition of the text in writing. Having someone read it aloud to you would actually replicate the experience of recording miscues a little better than just reading it silently, since you'd be trying to catch the miscues as they occur, rather than looking back and forth between the text and the reader's version. The answers are at the end of the chapter; you might want to do all five sentences before you look at the answers so that you won't peek at an answer too soon.

The first two examples come from Elaine, a fourth-grader.

1. Text: That's not a very big house for a dragon.
   Elaine: That's not a very big horse for a dinosaur.

2. Text: Henry didn't think he wanted to take care of a pet.
   Elaine: Henry don't, didn't, didn't think he wunded to take care of a pat.

The next three examples come from Sarah.

3. Text: Oh, and the next two hours tripped by on rosy wings.
   Sarah: Oh, and the next two hours tripped by on a, tripped by on rosy wings.

4. Text: There was no other like it in any of the stores . . .
   Sarah: There was nothing else like it of any of, in any of the stores . . .

5. Text: But whenever Mr. James Dillingham Young came home and reached his flat above he was called "Jim" . . .
   Sarah: But whenever Mr. James Dilligram Young came home to reach his flat above he would call "Jim."

Go ahead and check the answers now. If there are any you did differently from mine, think about why I marked them the way I did. It's not a bad idea to have someone read aloud to you and do a little practice on doing these basic miscue markings, getting a good handle on them before you look at the ones in the next section. What you've learned at this point will enable you to transcribe the vast majority of miscues.

Recording miscues: Some additional symbols and conventions

As we saw once we moved on from simple substitutions, omissions, and insertions, miscues often involve more than one word. A miscue may affect not only the structure of a sentence as a whole but its relationship to the following sentence as well. Also, there are ways to flag other kinds of information about miscues that may be useful for us to think about.

A simple example is the recording of pauses. If a pause lasts more than about five seconds, it's useful to record it, and perhaps indicate its length (another good use of the audiotape). Pauses are, typically, a sign that a reader has gotten stuck; if followed by a miscue, they tell you that the reader was probably actively thinking about what came next. Here's an example of how they're marked, with an elongated *p*:

[from Elaine's reading] . . . "To have the dog sit up and p/ shake hands.

Intonation miscues

Sometimes we see a miscue where all the words are read just fine, but the intonation is off; perhaps a sentence is read so that it sounds like two, or two sentences are run together. Take a look at Darcy's miscues here:

... I replied, "Chocolate, food you eat it, it's a present."

Her first miscue here is represented as the omission of a comma. Remember that we saw earlier how punctuation acts as an indicator of the syntax of written language? In this case, the commas show the speaker's utterance broken into four short bursts, each one standing on its own. Darcy ran together "food you eat," and then omitted the word *it* since it had no place in this new sentence structure. (Of course, the unusual syntax of this passage is because it represents speech, which often is punctuated to reflect oral language rhythms rather than the more formal conventions of written communication.)

Here are a couple of miscues of this type for you to practice on.

6. Text: Streams of meltwater flow on the ground. After nearly six months of winter, at last it is spring.
   Miranda's reading: Streams of meltwater flows on the ground after nearly six months of winter, at least it is spring.

7. Text: Henry got a shoe box and made holes in the lid. He wrote Dragon House on the box.
   Elaine's reading: Henry got a shoe box and made holes and, in the and he were, went Di-, wanted Dinosaur Horse on a box.

Intonation miscues can also occur on a single word, where they usually involve putting the stress on the wrong syllable. There's plenty of room for differences in the ways that various people pronounce a word, but an intonation miscue should be marked if the part of speech is changed (*PROject* as a noun changed to *proJECT* as a verb), or if it sounds like a definite mispronunciation, especially of a word you think the reader might not know. For instance, Darcy, a Canadian, read "VERmont" for *Vermont*: she probably didn't know the word but made good use of phonics in figuring it out.

Language variation miscues

Every speaker of English speaks his unique version of the language, which is molded by the community he grew up in: its country, region, and town; its social class makeup; its greater or lesser influx of people from other areas. Our language is also affected by when we live—our generation—and the kind of work we do, both of which carry their own special vocabularies.

Versions of English may typically use different words than one another to express the same idea. However, these variants are often too dissimilar to turn up as miscues. A teenager or young adult reading "I was incredulous" is unlikely to read it as "I was like, 'Hel-LO'!" even if that's what she'd be likely to say herself. But word pronunciations do vary from one group to another, and will show up in miscues. However, are they really miscues? They may only even be noticeable if the listener and reader speak different versions of English.

Let's take the word *lieutenant*. In the United States, when a reader says "lootenant," the teacher wouldn't call it a miscue. In Britain and Canada, the same would be true for the student that reads "lefftenant." But what if a British teacher is listening to an American reader, or vice versa? Is the unexpected pronunciation marked as a miscue? It is, I hope, pretty clear that it's not. You may want to note a pronunciation different from your own if you have a particular reason for wanting to remember it, but if the word is pronounced the way the reader would say it in everyday speech, it's not considered to be a miscue.

Another example comes from Miranda's reading a book about arctic wildlife; she consistently read the word *arctic* as "artic." Even if you, as the teacher, always pronounce the first *c* and think of Miranda's version as inaccurate or annoying, it's still not a miscue. Her pronunciation makes it clear that she knows what the word is, since she's saying it exactly the way she would if she were talking about the Arctic.

Another example would be a child who reads *rabbit* as "wabbit" because his speech is still immature. That may be an issue for the speech and language specialist, but it's not a miscue. (Again, you might still want to mark it if you wanted it to remember it, but it wouldn't be treated as a non-word substitution.)

Particular groups in the same country may vary somewhat in their pronunciations of particular words. An African American student may read *asked* as "axed," a Bostonian may read *park* as "pahk," a Southerner may read *cat* as "cay–et." None of these is a miscue; indeed, you probably wouldn't even notice them if you spoke the same version of English as the speaker.

Students whose first language isn't English may also pronounce words differently than the teacher does. A little knowledge of the sound system of the reader's first language can increase your awareness of what differences are likely (such as a Spanish-speaker's substituting *b* for *v* and vice versa in English words). However, there's an easy rule of thumb: If the reader pronounces a word the way she would when speaking, it's not a miscue.

This is an extremely important point, since some versions of English have lower status than others and indeed may be stigmatized. However, in doing miscue analysis, we're not thinking about whether a reader pronounces words in a way that would be seen negatively in a job interview, or that reflects that he speaks English with an accent; the issue is whether he knows what he's reading. Remember, if a British teacher counted it as a miscue if you read *schedule* as "sked-jul" (rather than "shed-yule") you'd feel that you were being misinterpreted. It's the same for a child who says, and reads, "dess" for *desk*. Not a miscue.

When miscues due to language variation affect word choice or sentence structure rather than just pronunciation, they're marked and coded as miscues, since they're a deviation from the text. (Different pronunciations are just an alternative rendition of the text.) Examples of this kind of miscue are an American's inserting *the* into a British sentence where someone is "in hospital," or a midwesterner's replacing *on* with *in* when the text is a New Yorker's "stand on line." However, as we'll see later in the analysis of miscues, we do take the student's version of English into account in thinking about his effectiveness as a reader.

How important is this marking system?

The purpose of these conventions of marking miscues is to be able to reconstruct the reader's interaction with the text. Period. They don't involve, at this point, any analysis; nor do they for the most part reflect a particular theoretical perspective. Since the way that miscues are marked is the most immediately visible part of an approach to looking at oral reading, it's sometimes seen as more central and important than it is. For instance, teachers talking about running record and miscue analysis might say that the biggest difference between them is that a running record can be done on a blank sheet of paper or a form, where for miscue analysis, you need a copy of the text.

However, the marking system itself is a relatively trivial part of the process. *Every* method of recording miscues is trying to reproduce what the reader did, with the usual tradeoffs between efficiency and precision. Miscue analysis, with its focus on getting a relatively complete and complex picture of the reader, especially emphasizes detail and accuracy. In miscue analysis we're trying to get a full picture of what the reader does; the central tool that we begin with, therefore, is a marking system that can replicate everything the reader said.

In the next chapter, we'll go on to what happens immediately after the reading, prompting the reader to retell what she's read.

Answers to marking practice

1. That's not a very big **horse** house for a **dinosaur** dragon.

2. Henry **didn't** didn't think he wanted to take care of a **pat** pet.

3. Oh, and the next two hours tripped by on **a** rosy wings.

4. There was no other **nothing else** like it in any of the stores . . .

5. But whenever Mr. James **Dilligram** Dillingham Young came home and **reach** reached his flat above he was **would call** called "Jim" . . . OR

   But whenever Mr. James **Dilligram** Dillingham Young came home and reached his flat above he was **would** called "Jim" . . .

6. Streams of meltwater **flows** flow on the ground. **After** After nearly six months of winter, at **least** last it is spring.

7. Henry got a shoe box and made holes **and** in the lid. **and he** He wrote **Dinosaur Horse a** Dragon House on the box.

   1. were
   2. went Di-
   3. wanted

7

Conducting Good Retellings

A miscue analysis *always* includes a retelling by the reader, since we need to know what she understands from her reading as well as what her miscues are like. Since teachers often underestimate how much a reader can get out of a text even despite many miscues, a retelling helps ensure that we base our assessment of the reader on a full range of evidence.

It's important that the retelling be student-centered, so that we can discover the meaning of the text as the reader sees it, not in response to preset questions. Also, remember how we saw from the mardsan giberter story that just because you can answer comprehension questions doesn't mean that you've understood what you've read. An open-ended retelling goes deeper.

In the version of miscue analysis that we're using here, there isn't any provision for assigning a score for retelling or comprehension. Unlike an informal reading inventory, where responses to questions are used to assign a reader to appropriately leveled material, the purpose of a retelling in miscue analysis is to gain a holistic sense of the reader's understanding, to give us a window into another aspect of the reading process. (There is, however, a procedure for scoring retellings in the more elaborate Procedure I of miscue analysis: See Goodman, Watson, & Burke, 1987. It involves preparing a story outline and making sure that your questioning touches on the points covered in the outline.) In Chapter 9, I'll talk about how to assess and summarize what we learn through retellings; here the focus will be on how to carry them out.

Although the retelling is student-centered, it doesn't mean that the teacher doesn't take an active role. A good retelling is an active interchange in which the teacher attends to the reader's responses and encourages her to expand on them, as well as asking probing questions that explore some of the reader's miscues as well as picking up on what we've learned about this reader through ongoing work with her.

A retelling can be brief or it can be longer. The first time you work with a reader, or when you're doing a more formal assessment, you'll want to take enough time to explore multiple aspects of his comprehension, and to investigate how some of his miscues affected his understanding. In ongoing work with a reader, you might choose to focus on one aspect of understanding, such as character development or a complicated aspect of the plot. However, a retelling should never be cursory; the point isn't to get the reader to quickly summarize the story to see if she got it or not, but to give the teacher an opportunity to (metaphorically) get inside the reader's head.

In helping you learn how to conduct a good retelling, I'll refer primarily to two that I've conducted. The first is Darcy's response to "A Sweet Trip on the Merritt." You should read the story in Appendix B if you haven't already, then read the retelling in Appendix C. I'll also quote several excerpts from Sarah's retelling of "The Gift of the Magi." If you're not familiar with this classic O. Henry Christmas story about a wife who sold her hair to buy a fob chain for her husband's watch, while her husband had sold his watch to buy combs for her hair, it's widely anthologized and can also be found on the Internet at http://www.promo.net/pg.

Unaided retelling

A retelling always begins with the reader's unassisted recounting of what he remembers. You can use a simple prompt, using phrases like, "Tell me what you remember," "Tell me everything you recall about what you read," "Tell me in your own words about the story." Some readers will say more than others. Darcy just said, "I can't really, you know, explain it all that well," and needed lots of prompting to go further, while Sarah answered at length, and quite accurately, before I made any further comments:

> Okay, it was about this lady who wanted to get her husband a Christmas gift but she didn't have enough money. So she sold her most prized possession, which was her hair, so that she could get money to buy him a Christmas gift. Then, when she went home her husband came home, and he was a little shocked that she had cut off her hair, and she was like, "Don't worry about it, don't worry about it," and she wanted to just open Christmas presents because she wanted him to know what she did for him. And when

she opened up hers, it was combs, which she couldn't really use because her hair wasn't long anymore. But she still wanted them, and really loved them, because they were probably from him. And then he opened his present and it was a chain for his clock that he always wore, and he had sold *his* clock which is *his* most prized possession to get *her* combs. So in exchange, they both sold something that was important to them to get the other person something. To make the other person happy.

(Her only mistake was reversing the order of the gifts' being opened.)

An important principle of unaided retelling is not to assume that just because a reader doesn't mention an element of the story, it doesn't mean he isn't aware of it. The unassisted retelling gives the teacher a sense of how the reader conceptualizes the story in her own words, but doesn't represent the limits of what she knows. At this point, the teacher's reactions are limited to nodding and making neutral comments like "Go on," "Tell me more."

Aided retelling

The next part of the retelling involves the teacher's prompting and probing to dig out more of the reader's understanding. My first question after Darcy's brief statement was to ask her to start by talking about the people in the story. As she continued responding, I sometimes built on what she'd said. For instance, when she said that the narrator had learned something about people's attitudes, I asked, "What about their attitudes?" Many of my questions were meant to get at different aspects of the story that she hadn't mentioned. For instance, "What happened when the guy got mad?"; "What kind of person do you think that he was?"

Usually what I'll focus on first in the assisted retelling is trying to get at aspects of the reader's understanding that she didn't volunteer initially. It's important not to introduce ingredients that the reader hasn't yet mentioned; for instance, rather than asking Darcy early in the discussion, "What about the people who went through the toll booth?", I asked "Were there other people in the story?"

Your questions should reflect, rather than correct, any of the reader's misconceptions. For instance, Sarah pronounced *magi* as "Maggie" every time she read it, so that's how I pronounced it in referring to it until I eventually told her the correct pronunciation. You might wonder if echoing readers' miscues and misperceptions is merely perpetuating them, but remember that the point is to *understand* the reader.

Then you may or may not want to clarify the point later; we'll see how I did this with *magi.*

There may be particular elements of story structure or literary understanding that you'd like to focus on in an assisted retelling. Appendix D shows a simple form (Board, 1976) that you can use to not only fill in comments about different story elements but remember to ask about them. However, this shows only one possible set of starting points. Think about your own purposes. If you're working with a student who doesn't understand that texts have authors who make particular choices, that's an area you might want to always include in retellings: "Why do you think Beverly Cleary decided that Ramona would have problems with spelling?" If you're doing a biography unit with your class and use a brief biography for a miscue analysis, a good retelling question would be "How did event X affect this person's life?" A retelling of a nonfiction passage could be guided to focus on, for instance, ideas and supporting evidence rather than story structure.

You can use a form to plan a more focused aided retelling. When I did Darcy's miscue analysis, I used the form seen in Appendix D to construct a retelling guide for this particular story, to help me monitor and probe for her understanding of details (Figure 7–1).

This filled-in retelling guide makes explicit what I was generally aware of while talking to Darcy: It's clear that she understood and remembered virtually every important element of the story; she was a little slow sometimes in recalling particular details, but otherwise had as good an understanding as one could ask for.

Probing of miscues and misunderstandings

One of the most interesting aspects of conducting a retelling is the opportunity it gives us to understand the extent to which readers did or didn't understand the readings they'd produced with their miscues. I'll share two examples at length, both involving repeated miscues on the same word.

Elaine's dinosaur

Elaine, in June of third grade, read aloud the story "Henry's Choice." David, a doctoral student, conducted the retelling. The story is about a boy who wants a pet, builds a dragon house, and says he's going to catch a dragon. Eventually he goes out and brings back what he says is a dragon. His grandfather tells him it's a lizard. Henry, after agreeing, says, "But it looks like a dragon."

Text Features	Text Information		Inferences beyond the text; other comments
Characters-who	✓ Fred (narrator) Other toll collectors ✓ Drivers	✓ Children ✓ Businessmen ✓ Supervisor ✓ People he meets later	
Characters-development	✓ Fred-friendly ✓ Drivers - vary in reactions		*Fred was "nutty"; I wouldn't do that!"*
Story line	✓ Fred takes job at toll booth. ✓ The job is a pleasant one. ✓ One day, he accidentally gives an M&M with a driver's change. ✓ He begins giving them out on purpose. ✓ He describes people's reactions— cheerful, neutral, suspicious. ✓ He nearly gets in trouble with his supervisor. ✓ People he meets later recognize him.		*Wasn't sure about why he liked the job.* *Didn't remember this at first, but then she did.*
Underlying Plot	✓ Gave M&M's to 25,000 people		
Inferences about themes, etc.			*Fred learned something about people and their attitudes; they react differently, but most are friendly.*

Figure 1. Retelling Form, Adapted from Board, 1976.

The words *dragon* and *dragons* appear twenty-two times in this brief story, mostly in the second half of the text. Elaine's first reading of *dragon* was "danger"; then her next five readings were correct. Then she read the following two sentences. (You saw them earlier, in Chapter 6.)

Text: Henry got a shoe box and made holes in the lid. He wrote Dragon House on the box.

Elaine's reading: Henry got a shoe box and made holes and, in the and he were, went Di-, wanted Dinosaur Horse on a box.

She read *dragon* as "dinosaur" the next fourteen times it appeared. Then finally, three lines from the end of the story, when Henry is saying that the lizard looks like a dragon, Elaine reads "di-, dinosaur, dragon." Then in the next, and final, line she reads that Henry got a "dinosaur" for a pet.

Talking with readers about repeated miscues like this one is a great opportunity to explore their evolving understanding of a text. Their original miscue may not make sense to them after a while, or they may persist with it and shape their understanding of the story to fit it.

Although Elaine didn't miscue on *dragon* every time she read it (only about three-fourths of the time), she began the retelling by telling David that the story was about "Henry's dinosaur." Later on in the conversation, David established that Elaine wouldn't want a dinosaur as a pet, and that they aren't around today. Then they had the following exchange:

David: Do you think there'd be dinosaurs running around that he could really find?

Elaine: Uh-huh [yes].

David: Where?

Elaine: The desert?

David: In the desert? Have you seen any dinosaurs in the desert?

Elaine: Yeah. [Elaine lived in the Sonoran desert in Arizona.]

David: You have! Real live dinosaurs. How big are they? How big? Very big, very little?

Elaine: They're small.

David: Small! Can we call dinosaurs by any other name?

Elaine: I don't know.

Although David didn't get any further in pushing this issue, the insight we can gain from this interchange is very valuable. We already knew that the problem wasn't an inability to read the word *dragon* since Elaine didn't make miscues on it at first. What the retelling tells us is that once she'd gotten *dinosaur* into her head, there was a plausible reason for sticking with it. Desert lizards or iguanas can easily be said to look like either dragons or dinosaurs. In fact, one could make a case that she didn't change the meaning of the story one bit, since it's about a child who tells everyone he's getting a mythical (or extinct) animal for a pet, but instead gets one that just looks like it. Hindsight suggests other questions David could have asked Elaine: "Did you notice that you didn't always say the same thing for this word?" But what's important here is the evidence that Elaine's repeated miscue represented a definite attempt to create and maintain meaning.

Sarah's Maggie

In Chapter 1, I shared Sarah's miscue of "Maggie" for *magi*, which I eventually helped her clarify. Let's take a look at some of our conversation about it. (I've made minor changes to make the wording more readable; excerpts are separated by ellipses.)

Sandra: Oh, the title. What do you think the title means? . . .

Sarah: See, I didn't get that, and I don't know why they called it The Gift of the Maggie. I still don't get why did they say Maggie, what's the Maggie? I didn't get that.

Sandra: Any ideas at all? Was there anything later in the story that gave you any hints about it?

Sarah: No, not really. Like the "gift" part, I got that. But I still don't know *who* the Maggie is, or *what* it is. They didn't really, like, say. It was just kind of like, "it."

Sandra: Right. Go ahead and take a look back. It's the paragraph that starts, "The Maggie, as you know"

Sarah: "Is the Wise Men." Oh, so they were like the people who brought, oh, so they were the ones who invented the art of Christmas, or something, or giving at Christmas?

Sandra: And what about *brought*, you were about to say they brought something?

Sarah: They brought gifts to the Babe.

Sandra: Do you know who "the Babe" is?

Sarah: I'm assuming that means like the baby Jesus, maybe? . . . Just because it says, "in a manger."

Sandra: Yeah, that would fit, wouldn't it? And that is right.

Sarah: It is?

Sandra: Yeah.

Sarah: Yeah, but are they saying that the Maggie, is that, like, supposed to be what these wise men invented? [It's] the name of what giving is?

Sandra: Okay, it's a little different than that. . . . The word that you read as "Maggie" is actually, it's pronounced differently but it means the same as the Wise Men. And it's a word that you don't hear that much anymore. And "Maggie" was actually a very good pronunciation for it. I could tell that you'd sounded it out. And do you ever remember hearing another name for the Wise Men, that the three of them were called?

Sarah: No.

Sandra: It's "magi."

Sarah: Oh [laughing].

Sandra: Yeah. And so does that sort of all make sense?

Sarah: So it's like the gift of the Wise Men, is kind of what they're saying. *Ohhhhh!*

Sandra: Say more.

Sarah: Oh, I get it. So they kind of just like incorporated it into the whole, like, *thing.* So like, the Wise Men brought these gifts to the manger, but they're using a different, like . . . So are they . . . ? See, what I don't get is how does this have anything to do with the story?

Sandra: The magi part? Yeah. Well, what do you think?

Sarah: Well, 'cause like . . . Okay, this is like about this girl and this guy who, like, give up their most prized possessions to, like, give the other one something they thought they would like, right? Well, these Wise Men just gave this baby gifts. But it wasn't something like the baby was giving something up to give *them* something.

Well, she's got a point, doesn't she? Here's the final paragraph of the story:

> The magi, as you know, were wise men—wonderfully wise men— who brought gifts to the Babe in the manger. They invented the art of giving Christmas presents. Being wise, their gifts were no doubt wise ones, possibly bearing the privilege of exchange in case of duplication. And here I have lamely related to you the uneventful chronicle of two foolish children in a flat who most unwisely sacrificed for each other the greatest treasures of their house. But in a last word to the wise of these days let it be said that of all who give gifts these two were the wisest. O all who give and receive gifts, such as they are wisest. Everywhere they are wisest. They are the magi.

O. Henry is suggesting that the magi initiated the giving of Christmas presents, but that Della and Jim, by sacrificing to give, are the true spiritual descendants of the magi. But to a young reader in today's highly secular culture, where Biblical references aren't common in public discourse the way they would have been in 1906, the analogy must seem a little forced.

What does this interchange tell us about Sarah as a reader? She actually did pretty well with *magi*. She came up with a reasonable pronunciation of it, and the correct pronunciation wouldn't have added anything since she didn't know the word. Although she was puzzled about what this "Maggie" had to do with the story as a whole, a story she did understand, once she realized it referred to the Wise Men, she not only grasped the author's point but had a critical response to it.

As for my role, notice how I referred Sarah back to the text and asked her in different ways to try to figure out what the "Maggie" were. It was only when I felt she'd reached a dead end in what she could figure out for herself that I told her what the word was. And of course the discussion didn't stop at that point.

Retelling as teaching and learning

As my discussion with Sarah about *magi* suggests, talking with a reader about her understandings and her miscues can provide opportunities for teachable moments. These moments can help readers learn something specific, like words they've miscued on, or help them discover new interpretations. Furthermore, such moments help students understand the reading process better and also help us see how they respond to instruction.

Also, students who are having problems with reading can particularly benefit from one-on-one instruction. Often a lesson that most members of a class benefit from will go right over the heads of these students; the material may be too hard for them, they may need a more focused interaction with one person to walk them through the idea or strategy, or both. When such students read aloud to you, even if you're not conducting a full-scale miscue analysis, it's extremely valuable to watch for miscues that will then lend themselves to some targeted teaching. You don't even have to be recording all the miscues if you make a mental note about, and perhaps jot down, any especially interesting ones.

Let's look at some examples of miscues and the teaching that might arise from them. (By the way, such teaching should only be done after the story has been read, as part of the retelling. It's crucial that the reading of the text not be interrupted.) The first few examples are all from Darcy.

Proper names

→

... the Greenwich toll station ...

1. Gr-
2. grĕn-
3. Greenwitch
4. Grenwitch

This is an excellent opportunity to talk about the reading of proper names. What's important here, of course, is only that the reader know that the word refers to a particular toll station on a particular parkway. To someone who doesn't know the area, the station name itself doesn't have any meaning. Although Darcy produced an excellent rendition of the word through her use of graphophonic knowledge, she also could have decided to just think of it as the "G toll station" and keep reading. When we're stuck, there's always a trade-off between trying for accuracy and trying for speed, an excellent concept to discuss with students.

Corrections

Here are two of Darcy's miscues:

ⓒ bought
I brought a radio to work every day.

ⓒ actually
[I] accidentally gave one to a driver with his change.

In both cases, Darcy miscued, read ahead a little, and then corrected herself. You could ask her to describe when she realized she should go back, and why. Readers often assume that they should correct everything that they haven't read exactly as written, but of course Darcy's first miscue changes the meaning and doesn't work with the rest of the sentence, while her second one works grammatically and changes the meaning only slightly. This is another good chance to talk about the trade-off between speed and accuracy. Another good example to share with Darcy at this point would be her following reading:

I'd   who'd
I've even picked up hitchhikers who had gone through my

booth.

These minor, uncorrected miscues are a good example of the kinds of changes that don't need to be fixed at all.

Hard words

In Sarah's reading of "The Gift of the Magi," many of her miscues that didn't make sense were on difficult words that she almost certainly didn't know. Here are some examples:

implication ₴ *parmished-me*

the silent imputation of parsimony that such close dealing

implied.

(uc) ₴ *mendacy*
mendis—

... on the lookout for the mendicancy squad.

₴ *long-itudinal*

... a rapid sequence of longitudinal strips.

₴ *scurrentstiny*
₴ *scurrentsy*   ₴ *insequential*

Let us regard with discreet scrutiny some inconsequential

object.

coracle

... the uneventful chronicle of two foolish children.

During the retelling I had some interchanges with Sarah about hard words and how she dealt with them. Early in our conversation, when she said she didn't really understand the story at first, we had the following exchange:

Sandra: I was noticing too that the first couple pages had a lot of very challenging words; do you think that's part of why you didn't get what was going on at first?

Sarah: I think that I didn't get what was going on because I was concentrating, I was trying to make sure I didn't miss anything, but then it's kind of hard when you, like I sound out words, so it's hard to stop, sound out a word, and then remember what you're reading. See, I have to keep going, . . . I read over, and make sure I get it.

This shows that she had a good sense of the trade-off between speed and accuracy, and that she had a strong instinct to keep going, in order to preserve the meaning of the story as much as possible. Her comment also reinforced my sense that she was using phonics almost exclusively to figure out the unknown words, rather than using a strategy of, for instance, consciously substituting a word that would make sense.

Later in the retelling, I returned to the issue of challenging words. I asked her to reread the "imputation of parsimony" sentence:

Sarah: [reading] "Pennies saved one and two at a time by bulldozing the grocer and the vegetable man and the butcher until one's cheek burned with silence impoli-, impotation of parminshy, parmishy that such close dealing implied."

Sandra: So, what did you do when you came to those words?

Sarah: I usually just sounded out by going one sound at a time, but it's hard because the English language is a bunch of different languages mixed together.

Sandra: Exactly!

Sarah: So this *u* can be making "uh," or a "u" sound, and all different letters can make different sounds, so it's kind of hard to tell which sound they make. So that's what makes it hard.

Sandra: And generally, how do you think you did on sounding out those hard words?

Sarah: Like on the words I think I did really well. Some of them like these were really hard, like ones I've never seen before. Usually if I've seen them, I can at least get somewhere close.

Sandra: Yeah, and I think one of the tricky things when you are reading and you come to a hard word, you have to think, "Well, is this a word I know, but I've just never read it before, I've never seen it in print, or is it a word that I don't know at all?" And one of the things I was noticing all the way through, I agree you did do a good job of sounding out. I think sometimes you did get them right. You really had to work at them, and I think [with] just about all of them you came real close.

My contribution here was primarily to reinforce that she was doing okay, as well as highlighting her idea that words you've never seen before offer a different challenge than words that might be part of your vocabulary. I also could have suggested that she just say "blank" and keep going if she came to a word that she was pretty sure she didn't know, realizing that this would help her maintain her speed and focus on meaning. Also, sometimes further context helps illuminate a word that was unclear before.

I followed up by asking Sarah if she had any idea what "imputation of parsimony" meant. She realized that the butcher and other shopkeepers were angry for some reason, but wasn't quite sure why:

Sandra: And why [were they mad at her]?

Sarah: Because she kept bugging them, maybe.

Sandra: Yeah, and what do you think she was bugging them about?

Sarah: That's what I don't know, like if she wanted to *work* there, if she wanted free food, or what? I don't know.

Then I realized that the lack of understanding wasn't because she had problems as a reader but because the social and economic context of this century-old story were unfamiliar to her:

Sandra: It's sort of another example of this story taking place almost a century ago now. It was probably something like she'd go to the vegetable man and buy some vegetables, and maybe say, "Oh, these carrots are a little limp, maybe could I have a couple cents discount or something?"

Sarah: Oh!

Sandra: And it's really so different today when you just go to the supermarket and pay what it costs.

Although I didn't say it explicitly, one of the messages that I hope Sarah picked up was that sometimes when you don't understand, it's because what you're reading is too hard in some way, not because you're a weak reader. What this episode told me was that despite her good use of phonics and her partial understanding of what was going on, the combination of two unknown words, a somewhat convoluted syntax, and an old-fashioned way of shopping made it pretty unlikely that she could have fully understood the sentence.

Strategies

One more example of teaching during a retelling comes from Miranda's miscue of "moscouts" for *mosquitoes* while reading about the Arctic. I've written about this elsewhere (Wilde, 1997) and will just summarize it here. When we discussed *mosquitoes* during the retelling, the best pronunciation she was able to come up with was "mos-quit-toes," which she admitted didn't sound like anything she'd ever heard of. The picture clearly showed a swarm of insects surrounding a bear, so I asked her what kinds of bugs might land on animals: "Mosquito. A tick. Ladybug . . . um . . . spider." It was only after a fair amount of interaction that she realized what the word on the page was; apparently, the *q* had thrown her off and she'd assumed that *mosquitoes* would be spelled with a *k*.

We then had this exchange, which was designed to get her thinking about a general strategy for cases like this:

Sandra: Does [what we did with this word] suggest to you anything about what to do when there's a particularly long word that you're stuck on?

Miranda: If you know it's a bug or you know it's an animal or something you can name some.

Sandra: Yes. And then look at [the text] and see if it makes sense.

These examples illustrate just a few of the ways that your interactions with students during retellings can serve a teaching function. The key is effective kidwatching (Goodman, 1978); when you understand something about why a particular miscue may have occurred, especially when it reflects an underlying strategy, you can then think, "How can I help her think about what she was doing here?" or "What's the next step for this reader?" It's important to realize, too, that teaching isn't just a chance to improve what readers are doing; it can also be a chance to help them realize what they're doing right. Miscues vary in quality (which we'll see more about in the next chapter), and those that don't affect the meaning don't need to be worried about or corrected. The concept of trade-off between speed and accuracy is an important one to share with students, and can be done while showing them in their own reading how a good, efficient pace will almost certainly lead to miscues, but it isn't a problem if those that damage the meaning are corrected. Readers of all ages tend to assume that word-perfect reading is best, but it just isn't true.

Retrospective miscue analysis

There's an important new teaching tool called retrospective miscue analysis; initially developed by Chris Worsnop (1980) it consists of asking readers to listen to the tape of their own miscues and helping them think about what they hear and further develop their strategies. There are a variety of ways to conduct retrospective miscue analysis; I strongly recommend the book *Retrospective Miscue Analysis: Revaluing Readers and Reading* (Goodman & Marek, 1996); its seventeen chapters by a variety of authors are a rich anthology of ideas for using readers' own miscues to help them learn and grow as readers.

I'll just share a couple of examples from Miranda's reading about the Arctic. I asked her to listen to the tape of her reading, with the book in front of her, and let me know when she heard a miscue or something interesting in her reading that she'd like to talk about.

After hearing herself read "plummage" for *plumage*, Miranda commented that she didn't know the word. When I asked her what her best guess would be, she said maybe it was the name of the animal. At that point I read the sentence back to her, using a placeholder for *ptarmigan*, which she hadn't figured out (other than knowing it was the bird in the picture): "A whatever-it-is in its white winter plummage." When I asked her to give me her best guess about the meaning of "plummage," she said, "the coat." I then talked with her about how we can figure out the meaning of a word we don't know by using the picture or the entire sentence.

When we came to her miscue of "cowves" for (caribou) calves, she asked for the tape to be stopped, then said, "I know it's like a baby caribou." She knew that a baby cow is called a calf, and said that more than one would be called "calfs." At that point I was able to tell her that she almost had it, that the plural is *calves*, which was the word in the book. Incredulously, she said, "But that's not a baby cow!" and I mentioned that they do have the same name. Along with exposing her to this little piece of information about language, our dialogue hopefully helped Miranda realize that her thinking was logical and she knew what the word meant. The only piece she hadn't grasped was that *calves* here was an unfamiliar (and therefore relatively unpredictable) extension of the meaning of a word she did know.

When we finished listening and responding to her tape of the reading, I asked Miranda if she felt she'd learned something from the session. She emphatically said yes, and although she wasn't able to put it into words at first, she said, "I know I learned something." Then she said, "Good readers, they kind of make, say a word wrong." I reinforced this by commenting that yes, being a good reader doesn't mean you get every word right.

I think you can see, even from these very few examples, that retrospective miscue analysis is a powerful tool since the reader herself chooses miscues to think about. I did quite a bit of teaching during this session, and you may have noticed how I tried to focus on what Miranda did right. Her reactions and body language as she listened to the tape made it apparent that she felt a little sheepish or embarrassed every time she heard a miscue. Students who have had problems with reading for years often have a very damaged sense of their own competence. By attending first to what they're doing right, we can help them be less critical of themselves and build some self-respect about their knowledge and strategies.

8

Coding Miscues
Procedures for Classroom Use

I hope that by this point you've gained a sense of how valuable it is to pay attention to what readers do. In this chapter you'll learn about a simple set of procedures that will help you think about each miscue and create a profile of the reader as a whole.

The procedures that we'll be exploring come from *Reading Miscue Inventory: Alternative Procedures* (Goodman, Watson, & Burke 1987). They make up Procedure III, a relatively simple form of miscue analysis that's appropriate for regular classroom use, including Title I and other remedial programs. One of the main reasons I've written this book is to make this powerful tool available to a wide audience. However, if you're interested in learning how to conduct more detailed miscue analyses, particularly for research purposes, I'd strongly recommend reading the Goodman, Watson, and Burke book and, if possible, taking a class in miscue analysis.

The form of miscue analysis you'll learn in this chapter enables the teacher to assess how effectively readers use syntactic information (sentence structure), semantic information (meaning), and graphophonic information (relating letters to sounds). It also documents the extent to which miscues have changed the meaning of the text. Retelling is looked at informally and holistically. Most of the information is coded at the sentence level, except for the analysis of phonics, where individual words are spotlighted.

Syntax, semantics, and meaning change

If you haven't already, please go to Appendix E to read Darcy's rendition of "A Sweet Trip on the Merritt." We'll be using it to learn the coding system, and I'll excerpt parts of it here as necessary. Notice that each sentence is numbered.

The first step in analyzing the reader's miscues in Procedure III is answering three questions about each sentence. (All descriptions of aspects of Procedure III have been taken, with some adaptations, from Goodman, Watson, & Burke, 1987.) These three questions refer to syntactic acceptability, semantic acceptability, and meaning change. We'll explore them one at a time.

General procedures for coding sentences

We'll primarily use Darcy's miscues to help you learn the coding system. "A Sweet Trip on the Merritt" has seventy-six sentences and Darcy had miscues in thirty-eight of them, or exactly 50 percent. The coding system does, however, tabulate data for all the sentences in a reading, not just those with miscues. (In practice, if the story is a long one, you don't necessarily have to code the whole thing, just a representative chunk. If you code just part of the story, I'd suggest at least twenty-five to fifty sentences, beginning partway into the story, after the reader's had time to get the feel of it.)

The first step is to number the sentences, and the coding is then done, usually, on the right-hand margin of the copy where you've recorded the miscues. You can look at Appendix F, which is Darcy's reading after all the coding has been completed, to see how this looks. You can summarize your results on the coding sheet that appears as Appendix G, which you can then save in the student's folder. All sentences are coded so that we can assemble a profile that takes into account how well the student processed a text as a whole; weak miscues obviously have a much bigger impact if they occur in 40 percent of sentences as opposed to 5 percent.

Also, we code each sentence based on the reader's rendition of it *after all corrections have been made.* This is a crucial point. What we're trying to capture is the extent to which the reader has been able to construct meaning as he reads. Self-correction is a tool for preserving or regaining meaning after it's been compromised by a miscue, a tool that good readers use productively. (Of course, readers also self-correct even when a miscue does preserve the meaning, out of a natural tendency to want to "get the words right." This isn't a problem unless it's so compulsive that it slows the reader down quite a bit or interferes with reading for meaning.)

One other general principle to be aware of: Since coding miscues is a thinking process in which we make judgments about the linguistic acceptability of complex reading behavior, there will be ambiguities and judgment calls. You might feel that a reading of a sentence sounds a little bit off, but that it still sounds like an English sentence. Another person coding the same reading might decide it has sufficient problems to be called "not acceptable syntactically." The most important goal of miscue analysis is for the teacher to understand what the reader is doing and what her miscues mean. There's likely to be some variation in the way a particular miscue might be coded, but if you're consistent in the judgment calls you make, you'll be able to develop a sense of how different readers compare to each other and how readers change over time.

Syntactic acceptability: Does it sound like English?
(Spanish, or Chinese, or whatever language is being read)

In practice, teachers will usually do all the coding for a single sentence at the same time, but here we'll deal with each coding question separately before putting them together.

In asking whether a student's reading of a sentence is syntactically acceptable, we're looking to determine the extent to which she's able to preserve the basic grammatical structure of the text. A good reader will typically be brought up short if a sentence doesn't sound like a sentence, and will probably try to correct it. A weaker reader, or one grappling with a text that's syntactically too complex for him, may keep going, or perhaps be unable to correct a miscue that damages grammaticality.

Let's code some miscues for syntactic acceptability to see how this question works. As always, the teacher's thinking process is the most important part of why you're doing this. Doing the coding is the avenue for reflecting on the nature of the miscues and any corrections of them.

Syntactically acceptable because miscues were corrected.   Darcy didn't have any strong examples of this, so I'll use one from Sarah. Here's her reading:

Della finished her cry and attended to her ⓒ which ⌐cheeks⌐ with the
rick - la la la la la.
powder rag.

Up until the "la la la," her sign that she realized the sentence wasn't coming out right, Sarah had produced a sentence that wasn't grammatically acceptable. Two indications of this: It just doesn't sound like a sentence, and she'd changed the part of speech of a word. *With* begins a prepositional phrase; when it's changed to "which," it sounds like the beginning of a new clause, leading you to expect another verb after *rag*. When she saw a period instead, Sarah presumably realized that something was off and so corrected it. Because of the correction, then, her reading of this sentence would be coded as syntactically acceptable. It's the final version that counts.

Syntactically acceptable despite uncorrected miscues.   Since readers have a strong impetus to ensure that what we read sounds like language, they may leave miscues uncorrected as long as the result is grammatical. Often these miscues vary the author's phrasing in minor ways. Some examples from Darcy are sentences 10 and 12:

out   of-

On breaks we usually went in the back room of the building

at the side of the road.

It's
It was a 20-cent toll.

Such miscues can also be somewhat complex, such as sentence 54:

To which I replied, "Chocolate, food you eat it it's a present."

Darcy did actually alter the syntactic structure. Three phrases, *chocolate, food, you eat it*, were changed to two: "chocolate, food you eat." But the important point is that her reading still sounds okay. A good rule of thumb is to read the sentence aloud, with the reader's miscues (after all corrections), and see if it sounds like English. In borderline cases, reading the sentence aloud to others and getting their input may help you decide.

These uncorrected miscues didn't change the meaning except in the most minor ways, but a sense of language structure can be preserved even when the miscue doesn't work in other ways. Let's look at sentence #48, which has several miscues.

computer
On Hiroshima Day during the morning commuter traffic,
prosperious
pros-
I was merrily doing my job until a prosperous-looking

ak-
executive went through my booth and jammed on his brakes.

Darcy's use of "computer" for *commuter*, although not fitting the meaning as a whole, still sounds perfectly good in terms of sentence structure. Even though her miscue of "$prosperious" for *prosperous* isn't a real word, it "feels" like an adjective. In fact, non-words can often, if not usually, be assumed to work at the grammatical level unless there's some reason to think otherwise, such as leaving off a crucial suffix.

Not syntactically acceptable.   I judged only two of Darcy's sentences to be unacceptable in terms of grammatical structure, 22 and 68:

I got to know a lot of people ⟨uc⟩ in as close a relationship ⟨c⟩ as

1. as
2. in a cl—
3. as a close

I could be achieved in about four seconds.

with the Goddards   *day*

During this vacation I stayed at Goddard College a few days.

In both cases she got somewhat tangled up on more than one word. In her unsuccessful attempt to grapple with the phrase *in as close a relationship*, she ended up omitting the preposition *in*, which was necessary for the sentence to work. However, you don't need to be able to describe what's going on grammatically to realize that her reading of the sentence is problematic. You need only read her version after all her corrections: "I got to know a lot of people as a close relationship as could be achieved in about four seconds." Reading the student's version aloud is, again, an especially good way to use your own sense of language to make a judgment about syntactic acceptability.

The structure of the "Goddard College" sentence isn't as badly damaged in Darcy's reading, but I would call it grammatically unacceptable because of the phrasing "a few day." (This is, however, a good example of a judgment call. One could make a reasonable case that this is too minor a syntactic problem to make the sentence as a whole ungrammatical.)

For a very clear example of how a small miscue can create a nongrammatical sentence, let's take a look at Miranda's sentence that we saw in Chapter 4:

from

Musk-oxen form a protective circle around their young.

Her little miscue made a big difference; by replacing a verb with a preposition, she created something that just wasn't a sentence. As a rule, if a miscue changes the part of speech of one or more words, there's a reasonable chance that it's created a structure that doesn't work as an English sentence.

Whose grammar are we talking about?   In talking about syntactic acceptability, it's crucial to realize that we're talking about the reader's version of English. There's an underlying grammar of a language that all of its speakers share, as well as surface features that differ from one group to another. As we saw in Chapter 6, miscues sometimes occur when one reads a text written by an author who speaks (or represents in dialogue) a different version of English. For instance, if an American teacher reads aloud a book by a British author, or a teacher from the northern part of the United States reads aloud from a book where the characters speak in a strong Southern style, some of the reader's sentences may sound like a mixture of the author's English and her own, as she both attends to the text on the page and filters it through her own version of English.

In some cases, the text differs from the reader's English because it's more literary-sounding than ordinary spoken language, as in Sarah's reading:

"Dell," said he, "let's put our Christmas presents away . . ."

A miscue that translates the author's syntax into the reader's is a positive sign that meaning is present for the reader. Why else would such miscues occur? You might want to try reading aloud (and rapidly enough to make miscues) a children's book, particularly one with dialogue, whose language is somewhat different from your own, to see how natural it is to shift toward one's own version of English. Try it with this passage from *The Secret Garden* (Burnett, 1911). Read it aloud, quickly enough that you have some miscues, and see if they tended to happen at points where the language is different from yours.

> Mary flew across the grass to him.
> "Oh, Dickon! Dickon!" she cried out. "How could you get here so early! How could you! The sun has only just got up!"
> He got up himself, laughing and glowing, and tousled; his eyes like a bit of the sky.
> "Eh!" he said. "I was up long before him. How could I have stayed abed! Th' world's all fair begun again this mornin', it has. An' it's workin' an' hummin' an' scratchin' an' pipin' an' nest-

buildin' an' breathin' out scents, till you've got to be out on it 'stead o' lyin' on your back. When th' sun did jump up, th' moor went mad for joy, an' I was in the midst of th' heather, an' I run like mad myself, shoutin' an' singin'. An' I come straight here. I couldn't have stayed away. Why, th' garden was lyin' here waitin'!"

As we code readers' sentences for syntactic acceptability, therefore, what we're asking is whether the reading sounds like a sentence *in the reader's version of English.* Typically, this is most often challenged if the reader's English is different from the teacher's, and particularly if the reader's is a lower-status form of English. For instance, a reader who uses *ain't* in his everyday speech may well say it when reading. Similarly, of course, a reader who doesn't usually use this word may miscue "isn't" or "aren't" when the word in the text is *ain't*, as Sarah did:

aren't
I'm me without my hair, ain't I?

I won't attempt here to get into issues of whether students should be encouraged to acquire more prestigious versions of English (but see Perry & Delpit, 1998 and McWhorter, 2000). The point is that what we're measuring here is effectiveness as a reader, regardless of what version of English one speaks, and despite social attitudes about differences in usage.

Semantic acceptability: Does it make sense?

When we decide if a sentence containing miscues is semantically acceptable, we're looking to see if the student is reading in such a way that the text makes sense. As with miscues that disrupt sentence structure, good readers tend to notice when what they've read doesn't make sense and try to correct it. Since a sentence can't make sense if its structure isn't working, any sentence that's coded *N* for syntactical acceptability is also, automatically, coded *N* for semantic acceptability. You can see how this works for Darcy's sentence 22 and Miranda's muskoxen sentence. Without a sentence structure that holds together, the sentence as a whole can't make sense.

This doesn't mean, however, that the reader hasn't gotten anything out of the sentence, which is why retelling is so important. Over and over again, we find that even readers with many miscues that don't preserve syntax and meaning still have quite a strong understanding of what they've read. Miscues give us a sense of how meaning is and isn't being constructed during the reading process, but since oral reading is only a window on the entire operation, it's always possible that more is being understood than what the miscues suggest.

Let's now code some miscues of Darcy's for semantic acceptability.

Semantically acceptable because miscues were corrected. Just as we saw with syntactic acceptability, correction makes these sentences pretty obviously acceptable; we'll just look at one example, sentence 7:

©bought

I brought a radio to work every day and listened to my

favorite station, WBAI.

It doesn't make sense to have "bought a radio to work every day," but since the miscue was corrected, it's irrelevant to the coding.

Semantically acceptable despite uncorrected miscues. These are common. Sentences 25, 59, and 61 are typical examples.

Most of the people liked it.

I'd

I told him that I had decided to give out an M&M with the

change and that this was what had happened.

the   don't   here
He told me that public servants didn't joke around.

In every case, if you read them aloud, they make sense.

In many cases, if the reader mispronounces a proper name, or substitutes a similar name, it's considered semantically acceptable. This is because proper names are a special case. There's a lot of variability in how they're pronounced, and readers may miscue on them only because they've never heard them pronounced before, but the context makes the meaning clear. For instance, although Darcy made miscues on both *Greenwich* and *Vermont*, her pronunciation wouldn't hide the fact that Greenwich was the location of a toll plaza and Vermont a place where you can vacation.

Similarly, third-grader Bart read the name *Ferdie* as either "Ferdye" or "Freddie" the four times that it appeared in a story. I would consider this semantically acceptable since he was clearly reading it as the name of this particular character. (We'll come back to this example in talking about meaning change.)

However, you need to use your judgment on these. If I knew my class was familiar with the names of the planets and a student consistently read *Jupiter* as "Joo-PIE-der," I'd consider it semantically unacceptable, since there are only nine planets and Joo-PIE-der isn't one of them.

Syntactically acceptable, but not semantically. Non-words (other than proper names) make a sentence unacceptable semantically, pretty much by definition. We can see this in Darcy's sentences 38, 48, and 49:

¢ *constistuency*
Soon I acquired a whole constituency of regular customers.

computer
On Hiroshima Day during the morning commuter traffic, I

ⓤⒸ ¢ *prosperious*
pros-
was merrily doing my job until a prosperous-looking exec-

utive went through my booth and jammed ⓞⓝ his brakes.

Ⓒ *the*
He opened his door ⓐⓝⓓ came up to me and held up a red

¢ M-S-D
M&M.

A couple of comments: Notice that in sentence 48, the miscue that ensures the sentence doesn't make sense is "$prosperious"; the phrase *morning computer traffic* does have meaning.

The miscue of "$M-S-D" for *M&M* certainly is understandable since the word *LSD* appeared right below it on the page, but we do code it as semantically unacceptable since it has no meaning in English. However, this is an excellent illustration of why what's important is not so much the coding itself but the thinking it encourages us to do about the reader's process. In every case, we can think about why a particular miscue occurred. In this case, it's due to reading quickly so that the broader visual field influenced what she said. (Again, remember that the trade-off when one slows down to increase accuracy is that efficiency is decreased.)

I would imagine that it's also pretty likely that Darcy realized she'd made a miscue and that the word was really *M&M*, but that she decided to just keep going. Of course we have to just code the miscue at face value, but it's a good reminder that what we see isn't necessarily the full extent of what the reader understands.

Sometimes, by the way, a real word might just as well be a non-word, as in Sarah's miscue:

coracle
. . .the uneventful chronicle of two foolish children . . .

I discovered that a coracle is actually a type of boat, but of course Sarah was attempting to pronounce *chronicle* rather than substituting a similar word that she knew.

There are also sentences where only real words appear in miscues but the final result still doesn't make sense. I've found in practice that such miscues aren't very common; usually when a reading of a sentence doesn't make sense, it's because it's ungrammatical or contains a non-word; there are also many times when a miscue changes the meaning but still makes sense. However, when Miranda reads that a squirrel "makes" rather than "wakes" up, even though her reading isn't ungrammatical, it doesn't really make sense in this context. Similarly, I'd consider Sarah's repeated substitution of "Maggie" for *magi* to be a miscue that works grammatically but doesn't make sense, particularly since *magi* isn't capitalized in the story and is used as a generic rather than a proper noun. This was actually comparable to a non-word miscue.

Meaning change

When we've decided that a sentence is acceptable both syntactically (it sounds like a sentence) and semantically (it makes sense), then our third question is whether the meaning has been changed. Although this seems similar to the question about semantic acceptability, there's a subtle difference. What we're saying here is, "Okay, the reader produced a sentence that's grammatical and makes sense, *but*, despite this, was the meaning still changed somehow?" This question is therefore only asked when the first two questions are answered *yes*. In this case of meaning change, there are three possible answers: *N* if there's no meaning change; *P* (for partial) if there's minor meaning change; and *Y* if there's major meaning change. These distinctions obviously involve judgment calls, so as always what's especially important is consistency in your coding over time and thoughtfulness about what you're trying to understand and represent.

Miscues that result in no meaning change.   When a sentence is coded Y (syntactically acceptable), Y (semantically acceptable) and N (no meaning change), this is a sign that it's been read effectively. Of course, any sentence with no miscues in it is coded YYN, as is any sentence where all the miscues have been corrected, like Darcy's sentence 28:

Many people ~~wouldn't~~ notice until after they'd pulled out.
©didn't

However, a reader can also leave miscues uncorrected without changing the meaning of the sentence in any real way. The miscues are often small ones but may be more complex; Darcy's sentences 8, 70, and 26 show a range of examples:

The other toll collectors were some of the nicest and ^the^ most
I
interesting people that I've ever met.

I answered, "Well, I worked at a toll booth on the Merritt
was working   *© at*

Parkway this summer."

They would laugh and say thank you and maybe eat(the) one

or two M&M's that I gave(them).

Although there's a slight change of tense in sentence 70, it's so small in relation to the larger context that I don't consider it to have changed the meaning. Similarly, Darcy's reading of sentence 26 sounds a little awkward, but it's still grammatical, makes sense, and carries the same meaning.

Miscues that result in partial or minor meaning change. The only miscues of Darcy's that I considered to fall into this category were the ones where she slightly mispronounced *Greenwich* and *Vermont*. Although the sentences still made sense since it was clear that a place name was involved, the meaning was slightly changed since a listener wouldn't necessarily recognize that a specific real town in Connecticut and a New England state were being referred to. Of course, the reader may or may not have heard of them before; this would be interesting to explore in a retelling. Would the correctly pronounced *Greenwich* be as unfamiliar to her as her own "Grenwitch," or has she heard of the place but just didn't recognize it in print, perhaps because the *w* is silent?

Here are some examples from Sarah where the meaning was changed in fairly minor ways. I've included the entire sentence since that's the context for assessing meaning change.

[from Sarah's reading] Had King Solomon been the janitor,
with all his ~~treasures~~ *©treasured* piled up in the basement, Jim would

have pulled out his watch every time he passed, just to see
him pluck ~~at~~ *out* his beard from envy.

[from Sarah's reading] She looked at her reflection in the
mirror long, carefully, and ~~critically~~ *crucially*.

Miscues that result in major meaning change. It's a sign of Darcy's strength as a reader that none of her miscues in sentences that were grammatical and made sense changed the meaning in major ways. One sentence of Miranda's, however, definitely needed to be coded *Y* for meaning change:

wonder
Polar bears ~~wander~~ across the frozen sea.

Although the image is a charming one (visions of pensive big beasts!), the miscue does change the central meaning of the sentence.

The multiple miscues in one of Sarah's readings also changed the meaning of the sentence:

Dilligram *to*
But whenever Mr. James Dillingham Young came home and
reach *would call* *hug*
reached his flat above he was called "Jim" and greatly hugged
Mr. *Dilham*
~~by~~ Mrs. James Dillingham Young, already introduced to you

as Della.

Although Sarah's reading of the sentence contains nine miscues, only three of them work to alter the meaning. In changing the passive form *was called* to the active verb "would call," and reading *Mrs.* as "Mr.," she created a confusion about who was hugging whom.

One other example of meaning change: Although Bart's readings of "Fer-dye" or "Freddie" for *Ferdie* did make sense in the context of the story, I'd judge the one time he read "Freddie" to constitute a meaning change since it broke the consistency of his reading of the name.

In the next chapter, we'll see how these three coding questions work together and what they tell us. However, there's one more piece of coding to learn first, which fills in one final and central piece of what we want to know about a reader: the extent to which she uses graphophonic knowledge.

Graphic similarity

When a reader comes to a word he doesn't know, he can pronounce it as a whole, try to "sound it out" in smaller pieces, substitute a word that makes sense, say "blank" as a placeholder, and so on. Similarly, when a reader is going along fairly rapidly and makes a miscue perhaps even on a word she does know, we may see a miscue that's very meaning-based or one that's more closely tied to the letters on the page. For instance, Darcy's miscue of "computer" for *commuter* represents a very close link to the letters of the words, while her miscue of "didn't" for *wouldn't* seems driven more by meaning.

Teachers often misunderstand the value of looking at how readers use the graphophonic system. I find that a common response is to take *any* miscue as a sign of failure to use the graphophonic system: "If he was using phonics, he would have gotten it right." However, miscues happen. All readers make miscues, and error-free reading comes only at the cost of sacrificing speed and efficiency. Also, phonics is limited: It can't guarantee that we'll pronounce a word right, only that we'll come close. What's interesting, and important, is how effectively readers use this cueing system—the print on the page and its connection to sound—to construct meaning. As we'll see, a closer match doesn't always make for a better reading.

In Procedure III of miscue analysis, we look at each miscue that involves a single word substituted for another, in order to see how the reader has used the graphophonic cueing system. (Remember that when the reader has omitted or inserted parts of words like suffixes, these count as substitutions. Also, if the same substitution occurs repeatedly, only code it once so that it won't distort the data.) To do the coding, we determine how much graphic (visual) similarity there is between the word on the page and the miscue. The coding options are high (H), some (S), and no (N) graphic similarity. We code the first full miscue the reader made on the word (for instance, Darcy read "Gr-, Gren, Greenwitch, Grenwitch," so we code "Greenwitch"), whether or not it was eventually corrected. This coding is very different from the sentence coding since we're looking at words in isolation and want to see how the reader used phonics in his first stab at the word.

We're asking, therefore, how much the miscue looks like the text. To do this accurately, it's important to remember that we should spell non-words in a way that makes clear their relationship to the sound pattern of the text.

High graphic similarity

The easiest way to make judgments about graphic similarity is to think of the word in the text and the miscue as being divided into three parts: beginning, middle, and end. If two of the three parts look alike, the words are coded as having high graphic similarity. If one word is entirely contained in another, or there's more than 50 percent overlap, that would also be coded as "high."

Here are some examples from Miranda and Sarah:

High graphic similarity	
text	*miscue*
wander	wonder
plumage	$plummage
last	least
gradually	$gradly
Dillingham	Dilligram
doubled	doubted

In all of these miscues, one gets the sense that the reader's miscue has been very much driven by the letters in the word and the sounds that go with them.

Some graphic similarity

Miscues are considered to have some graphic similarity when one of the three parts (beginning, middle, and end) looks the same in the two words, or if the general configuration is the same, particularly for short words. I'd judge *at* and *in* to have some graphic similarity, even though they have no letters in common. Sometimes, too, especially for short function words with the same number of letters, the text and the miscue may share a letter but not in the same position; it seems reasonable to say that *the* and *him* have some visual similarity. These guidelines aren't necessarily written in stone, however; I tend to pay attention to my own instincts about whether the reader is strongly, somewhat, or not at all using visual cues in producing a particular miscue.

Here are some examples from Miranda and Sarah of substitution miscues that have some visual similarity to the text:

Some graphic similarity	
text	*miscue*
one	the
thousands	$thunsed
creature	character
agile	angle
read	said
peculiar	particular

In these miscues, the reader seems to be attending a little less closely to the print, perhaps skimming over the surface of the text a little more quickly. Of course, miscues with some graphic similarity may or may not work in terms of the meaning of the sentence, but we've already considered that question in the other sections of the coding.

Miscues with no graphic similarity

When the text and miscue share no letters in common and aren't highly similar in their configuration (such as number of letters), they're coded as having no graphic similarity. Here are examples from Miranda and Sarah:

No graphic similarity	
text	*miscue*
in	the
both	had
the	a
the	like
at	like
the	each

Looking at these miscues out of context, one might wonder why a reader would depart so far from the text. However, they're only a departure from the visual aspects of a text; they almost always occur when the reader is predicting a slightly different way of saying something than what the author has chosen. For instance, Sarah read:

There were two possessions . . . in which they both ~~took a~~ *had (R)*

mighty pride.

As in these examples, miscues with no letters in common with the text occur most often on function words, probably because they're short and we may not look as closely at them, plus there may be more room for variation than with content words like nouns and verbs.

Coding Darcy's miscues for graphic similarity

As I mentioned earlier, the easiest way to mark miscues for graphic similarity is right on the story itself, as you can see in Darcy's reading in Appendix E. However, to give you some practice in doing the coding, I've put all of Darcy's single-word substitutions in the following table so that you can try out the coding system yourself. (Remember: the choices are High, Some, or No graphic similarity.) My codings appear at the end of the chapter. If there are miscues where your answers differ from mine, think about why we might have disagreed. Since some of these codings aren't cut-and-dried but require judgment calls, your answer might be at least as reasonable as mine. The important point is that you understand why one would make a case for one coding rather than another.

Graphic similarity of Darcy's miscues		
text	*miscue*	*code*
for	at	
in	by	
Greenwich	Greenwitch	
brought	bought	
accidentally	actually	
could	I	
wouldn't	didn't	
working	work	
constituency	$constistuency	
up	by	
an	one	
commuter	computer	
prosperous	$prosperious	
his	the	
M&M	$M-S-D	
asked	said	
my	me	
what	that	
didn't	don't	
Vermont	VERmont	
days	day	
nowhere	it	
on	at	
at	in	
of	about	
I've	I'd	

This chapter has involved focusing on a great deal of linguistic detail, but in the next chapter we'll get to put the big picture together to see what the completion of a miscue analysis tells us about a reader.

Graphic similarity of miscues: Answers		
text	*miscue*	*code*
for	at	N
in	by	S
Greenwich	Greenwitch	H
brought	bought	H
accidentally	actually	H or S
could	I	N
wouldn't	didn't	S
working	work	H
constituency	$constistuency	H
up	by	S
an	one	S
commuter	computer	H
prosperous	$prosperious	H
his	the	S
M&M	$M-S-D	H or S
asked	said	S
my	me	H
what	that	H
didn't	don't	H
Vermont	VERmont	H
days	day	H
nowhere	it	N
on	at	S
at	in	S
of	about	N
I've	I'd	H

9

A Portrait of the Reader

Our coding of a reader's miscues has been a way of summarizing that then lets us generalize about her strengths, strategies, and possible future growth. In this chapter, we'll combine the data we've compiled about the reader's use of sentence structure, meaning, and phonics, as well as her retelling, into a comprehensive portrait. We'll walk through the procedures with Darcy's story; I'll then compare her reading to Miranda's and Sarah's, whose miscues and retellings you've seen pieces of.

The reader's construction of syntax and meaning (sentence level)

Now that you've learned what we're trying to understand from each of the three sentence-level coding questions, let's put them into practice on the first paragraph of Darcy's reading. We'll look at sentences #1–5, with my coding for each of them.

One summer I worked at a toll booth on the Merritt

Parkway.

I gave out M&M's with the change.

When a sentence has no miscues, it's simply coded YYN. Coding of sentences with no miscues can be done automatically since they don't reveal anything in particular about the reader. Do remember, of course, that readers don't use completely different strategies on sentences where they make miscues and those where they don't; it's just that their strategies aren't visible until they make a miscue.

©©
It all started when I was looking ©at for a summer job at a youth

by
employment agency in my hometown.

This sentence had three miscues. The first two were corrected and the third ("by" for *in*) doesn't make the sentence ungrammatical or meaningless. I'd code it YYN, but you could also make a case for YYP, since the third miscue suggests a very slight shift in location of the youth employment agency.

(UC) →

1. Gr—
2. Gren
3. Greenwitch
4. Grenwitch

They told me that the Greenwich toll station on the Merritt

Parkway needed employees for the summer.

As we've seen earlier with Darcy's miscue on *Greenwich*, the sentence is okay grammatically and semantically, but with a slight meaning change. I'd code it YYP.

The job sounded so unusual that I decided to take it.

No miscues, therefore YYN.

What I'd like to suggest is that, at this point, you turn to Darcy's uncoded story in Appendix E and code her sentences yourself, then compare your answers to mine in Appendix F. This will serve two purposes: You'll get some practice in coding rather than just reading my answers, and you'll build up a sense of Darcy's reading as a whole as you see what patterns emerge in the coding. Again, if any of your answers differ from mine, use this as an opportunity to think about why I reasoned as I did and whether your answer is also justifiable.

Summarizing the reader's use of syntax and meaning

The next step is to add up the totals for each question. The following table (see Appendix G for blank copies of the forms) has been filled in for Darcy's reading.

	Question #1 (syntax)		Question #2 (semantics)	
	number	*percent*	*number*	*percent*
Yes, acceptable	74	97%	71	93%
No, not acceptable	2	3%	5	7%
Total	76	100%	76	100%

	Question #3 (meaning change)	
	number	*percent*
No meaning change	67	94%
Partial meaning change	4	6%
Yes, major meaning change	0	0%
Total (count only those coded, not dashes)	71	100%

I'm sure you realized as you coded Darcy's sentences that she's an excellent reader. Although there were miscues in exactly half of her sentences, almost the entire story was grammatical and meaningful in her reading of it, with only a few minor meaning changes. Although these totals and percentages are a shorthand way of summarizing Darcy's reading, what's most powerful is the act of coding itself, since it leads you to think about what she's doing and why.

Summarizing the reader's use of visual cues

From the table we constructed at the end of the last chapter, you can make a similar tabulation for Darcy's use of graphic information in single-word substitutions.

A customary assumption would be that good readers make better use of phonics than weaker readers, and that therefore a greater percentages of miscues with high graphic similarity would be better, but this isn't the case. Non-word miscues, which undermine the meaningfulness of a sentence, typically have high graphic similarity, while Darcy's miscues with no graphic similarity were for the most part either corrected or didn't compromise the sentence:

Graphic (visual similarity)		
	Number	*Percent*
High	14	54%
Some	8	31%
None	4	15%
Total	26	100%

Out of ©ⁱ nowhere this girl came up to me . . .

about

. . . executives in New York City talked of some "joker" on the

Merritt Parkway . . .

It's not possible to state the ideal extent to which miscues should be visually similar to the text, since readers and texts vary widely, but as a general rule, effective readers do use the graphophonic cueing system in their miscues, but not slavishly or to the exclusion of other strategies. Most readers will have many miscues that are visually similar to the text, but good readers are likely to have more of a mix. Your sense of this will develop as you work with a number of readers, the same reader over time, or both.

Holistic, anecdotal descriptions of the reading and retelling

As the next step in creating a record of a reading episode, I'd recommend taking a few minutes to jot down your impressions of the student's reading of the text and your analysis of his miscues, as well as some summary statements about the retelling. Not only will this provide a useful record for the student's file (particularly for the retelling, which you probably won't transcribe), but it drives you to generalize based on what you've seen. As with so much of miscue analysis, the teacher's thinking is central and indeed the main point of the exercise.

Ideally, you'd write down some impressions about the reading and retelling during or immediately after the session with the reader, and then add further thoughts after you've coded the miscues. These descriptions needn't be at all lengthy; what's most important is to get the gist of who this reader is and what she's doing, as I've done here for Darcy.

THOUGHTS ABOUT THE READING

Darcy was clearly comfortable reading the piece, proceeding efficiently and self-correcting pretty consistently, especially when something didn't make sense. Coding her sentences, I saw that almost all her sentences "worked": she either had no miscues, the miscues were negligible, or she self-corrected. When a word was completely unknown to her, she tended to attempt it with phonics, but phonics didn't predominate as a strategy in general.

THOUGHTS ABOUT THE RETELLING

Darcy had a strong sense of the story in general and remembered many details of character and plot. Her sense of the story's theme was reasonable: that the narrator learned something about people and their attitudes.

By the way, there's one figure we haven't tabulated that you might have expected to: the percentage of miscues, or miscues per hundred words. The reason is that it just isn't very interesting. The number of miscues is more a result of the speed of reading, difficulty of the text for the reader, and so on. Also, there may be natural differences between people in the performance aspect of oral reading; I'm always impressed by how well news announcers do, since I, like many people, seem to trip over my tongue a lot. But this doesn't mean that I don't understand what I've read. Also, although fewer miscues has traditionally been taken to indicate a better reader, it could also indicate a reader who goes so slowly in order to avoid miscues that efficiency is sacrificed.

Comparing readers

To get a sense of what miscue analysis can show us about how readers differ from one another, I'd like to compare Darcy's profile piece by piece with profiles for Miranda and Sarah, both less successful readers. Let's look at their miscue profiles first.

In Figure 2, we see that Sarah had signs of being somewhat less effective as a reader than Darcy did, with Miranda less proficient still. (This does, of course, refer just to their experience with these particular texts; you'd never want to make high-stakes decisions about a student based on a single miscue analysis.) The fact that Darcy's substitution miscues showed less visual similarity to the text than did those of the other two girls is consistent with what we know about readers in general: Good ones use—but don't overuse—phonics, while weaker ones may rely too much on it.

	Darcy	Sarah*	Miranda
Question #1 -Syntactic Acceptability - Percentages			
Yes	97%	92%	78%
No	3%	8%	22%
Question #2 -Semantic Acceptability - Percentages			
Yes	93%	76%	49%
No	7%	24%	51%
Question #3 Meaning Change - Percentages			
No	94%	84%	83%
Partial	6%	11%	11%
Yes	0%	5%	6%
Graphic similarity - Percentages			
High	54%	76%	87.5%
Some	31%	20%	10%
None	15%	4%	2.5%

*Since the story Sarah read was long, I coded only 50 sentences.

Figure 2. Comparison of miscues for Darcy, Sarah, and Miranda.

Before we use my anecdotal notes about Miranda and Darcy to put these statistics in perspective, I'd like to point out a pattern that we can see across all three students. As long as a student is reading a text that she can cope with independently, even with quite a few miscues that don't make sense or that change the meaning of the passage, there are still many similarities across readers. Even with many weak miscues, most words are read without miscues and many miscues are either corrected or are "good" ones that don't damage the reader's understanding.

In cases where this isn't true, where readers are miscueing on every other word, they're attempting text that's way too hard for them, a pointless exercise since you can't see what their strategies are if they aren't able to connect enough with the text to make use of all the cueing systems of reading.

Also, all readers use visual information about the text through phonics, and most miscues will have high graphic similarity to the text, although typically less so for better readers.

Figure 3 shows my informal impressions of Sarah's and Miranda's readings and retellings.

Sarah	Miranda
Thoughts about the reading:	
Didn't let unfamiliar words or miscues slow her down much. Tried to get things right but would then keep going. Often produced non-words (but quickly) for unfamiliar words. Her sentences usually made sense when there weren't unknown words to deal with.	Used phonics to attempt unfamiliar words. A fair number of non-words. Didn't correct when things didn't make sense. Non-words made quite a few sentences not semantically acceptable.
Thoughts about the retelling:	
Retold at great length and accurately; good sense of the theme. Didn't understand the magi analogy at first since she didn't know the word, but then was able to react critically to it.	A good basic understanding of the text. Provided details when prompted. Eventually figured out *mosquitoes,* but needed lots of scaffolding. As she listened to her tape, she tended to assume all mistakes are bad.

Figure 3. Informal impressions.

Let's consider, then, what each reader's statistics mean in the context of what else we know about her.

Darcy was clearly an effective reader. Only 3 percent of the sentences in her reading (a mere two sentences) didn't work grammatically, and a few others didn't make sense. She used phonics but not excessively, and her understanding of the story was excellent. She was also efficient; she self-corrected but not compulsively, and often kept going if the miscue was minor. She's really a classic example of a good reader.

Sarah was a better reader than one would think from a first impression. Since the text was difficult, with complex sentence structure and a number of obscure words, 25 percent of her sentences didn't make sense, but this was most often because of using phonics on difficult words and coming up with a non-word. What's significant, however, is that only 8 percent of her sentences didn't work grammatically. She was able to retain sentence structure even when it was complex. She was able to retell the story at length; when she didn't understand parts, it was primarily because of the difficulty of the language.

Miranda was clearly a less effective reader than the other two, primarily because she often kept going when her reading wasn't making sense. Sometimes this was understandable, as when she was unable to figure out words like *ptarmigan* and *pasqueflowers,* but she'd also continue after making a substitution like "from" for *form,* which left the sentence with no verb. Many of her substitutions had high graphic similarity to the text, indicating that she relied heavily on a phonics strategy; she also needed a lot of scaffolding when trying out other strategies, as in my discussion of *mosquitoes* with her. She did, however, have a reasonable understanding of what she'd read.

If you take a look back at Figure 3, I hope you'll see how these comments mesh with the numerical data for each reader. Unlike informal reading inventories, miscue analysis doesn't assign labels to different ranges of scores; we can't say that students are excellent readers because they have some particular percentage of syntactically acceptable sentences or poor readers at some other percentage. This would be assigning a false precision to something that's complex and subtle. However, coupled with familiarity with the miscues themselves, the reader's retelling, and any other relevant information, the statistics compiled in Procedure III will give you a good sense of how a reader is using the cueing systems to construct meaning. Your sense of what the numbers mean will develop further as you work with different readers and with the same reader across time.

In the next chapter, I'll talk about what the next step might be in working with each of these readers and with readers in general.

10

What's Next for This Reader?
From Miscue Analysis to Instruction

gain, I'd like to use Darcy, Sarah, and Miranda as examples as we begin to look at how miscue analysis can inform our further work with a reader, as well as talking about some common patterns that we see across many readers and what these imply for teaching. Two guiding principles that I'll be focusing on are ensuring that the student has appropriate reading material, and working on strategies.

Building instruction on miscue analysis is a profoundly empirical approach, in that it grows out of what we see and hear about this particular reader, rather than a label or classification that's been applied to him. Rhodes and Dudley-Marling (1996) have made the important point that such categorizations, although often necessary for funding and assignment purposes, are generalizations that can't be assumed to correlate in every detail to everyone they're applied to: we have to look at the individual. Miscue analysis has been used with many, many kinds of students over the years. (See Weaver, 1994, for an excellent example of miscue analysis with a dyslexic student, and Brown, Goodman, & Marek, 1996, for a lengthy bibliography.) The power of miscue analysis comes from its insistence on rejecting a one-size-fits-all approach in favor of a scrupulous, caring attention to the individual.

What's next for Darcy?

Given Darcy's excellent reading, you'll probably be surprised to hear that she nearly failed seventh grade! She was a voracious reader of all kinds of texts such as *Mad* magazine and young adult novels, and her room was cluttered with the couple of hundred books that she owned. However, she tended to have a hard time dealing with the structures and requirements of school, with her assignments incomplete or late, I think often because they got in the way of her independent intellectual life as a reader.

Her reading was rapid and fluent, as we saw, and she wasn't overly picky about getting every word right or likely to waste a lot of time on words she didn't know. This efficient and sensible attitude contributed to her ability to read as many books as rapidly as she did and to love reading so much. Before we began the miscue analysis, Darcy said she was nervous because she knew she'd make a lot of mistakes. In my view, all she needed in the way of instruction was to be shown that her "mistakes" were actually desirable most of the time, since they helped her read more efficiently.

One might object that her poor grades were a sign of a problem, but that's another issue. As a reader, she was just fine; in fact, as a highly avid reader, she was better than just fine. Ironically, avid readers don't always do well in school, since it may distract them from the learning that they're really interested in. (I was like this myself in high school.) Therefore, perhaps another suggestion for working with Darcy and other students like her would be that her teachers work harder to engage such obvious intellectual energy, and to make school more flexible in letting her determine the direction of more of her own learning.

What's next for Sarah?

I met with Sarah in the summer before her senior year of high school. Because of some problems at birth, she had a mild to moderate hearing loss and had also been classified as having a learning disability and some other, perceptual, problems. She'd been in special education placements since second grade: pull-out in elementary and middle school and a separate track in high school. She did a moderate amount of reading on her own, and felt she read too slowly, so that it would take her a long time to finish a book. Reading was one of her stronger areas in school—she had greater problems with math—but she most likely wasn't at a level of reading where she could function well in a highly academic track. Her school, in an affluent area, had few appropriate options for students like her: Regular academic classes were quite rigorous, and the only other real option was special education. Her parents felt she wasn't being challenged enough in her special education track, where many of the students were less capable than her, so she was planning to spend her senior year in regular classes, including a consumer math class that was being offered by her school for the first time.

When I asked Sarah what she thought her strengths as a reader were, she said, "I usually can understand what I'm reading." She also said that she liked reading if she liked the story, and that she liked social studies and history. When I asked what she'd most like to improve, she said her speed as a reader.

Based on my hearing her read and talking with her, it was clear to me that Sarah's strategies as a reader were basically good, and that she had a pretty good awareness of what strategies she used, but that there was a definite developmental lag compared with other students her age, particularly in her high-achieving community. Since she didn't get many books read, and her special-education track wasn't very demanding (for instance, they had no homework), it's likely that she was falling further behind every year. Therefore, the goal that seemed to me to be most important for her, and that would also support her own goal of reading faster, was to get her to read, read, read: material that was interesting to her so that she'd want to stay with it and that was on the easy side so that she could build fluency and gradually work up to more challenging texts.

I approached this idea at several points in our discussion following the retelling. I asked if she read both fiction and nonfiction, and she said that she liked stories—fiction—best. Given her curiosity about history, I asked her if she'd ever read historical fiction; she hadn't. When I asked her what historical periods she'd find it worthwhile to read stories about, she had a very strong interest in "survivors of Nazi Germany," and mentioned that she'd always wanted to read *The Diary of Anne Frank*. (Her aunt and I went to a large bookstore with her later that day, and I helped her find a copy of the diary.) Later, when she mentioned that she'd like to be a teacher, possibly of grades 4–6, I suggested that a summer reading project for her might be to read historical novels written for adults and also some written for children, which would be a way to start learning more about children's literature.

I commented very directly to Sarah about the value of reading easy books. When I asked her if she had any questions for me, she said, "[for someone who's] in high school, and going to be a senior, is my reading okay?" I responded, "Maybe not quite as strong as the average reader your age. *But* the biggest key to becoming a better reader is lots of reading of stuff that's not too hard for you." I mentioned also that when you read easy material, particularly if there's a lot of it, you build up your speed and get to be a better reader generally. But if what you're trying to read is way over your head, you get bogged down, you don't understand, and you don't improve. So, I said, "Do whatever you can do to find stuff you're interested in reading and to make sure you're not reading stuff that's too hard." I suggested that reading a lot of easy, fun books over the summer would be a good way to prepare for the workload of her upcoming senior year in regular classes.

Although Sarah's strategies as they emerged in her miscues were mostly pretty good, I did spend some time talking with her about them. We saw some examples in Chapter 7, where I talked with her about how she dealt with hard words, including her use of phonics, as well as strategies she could try. Later in our discussion I asked her what she thought were good strategies when she got stuck or didn't know a word. She very sensibly replied, "Sound [it] out; keep reading and see if [that] helps you; if nothing else works, look it up in the dictionary." She also commented that when she read, she wanted to make sure that she didn't miss anything and that she understood what she was reading, so that her reading was sometimes slower than she would have liked.

I suggested that Sarah try an experiment; sometimes speeding up can help you understand better. (Thanks to Frank Smith, 1988, for this insight.) Once you get the rhythm of a piece of writing, the meaning often falls into place. Since her non-word miscues tended to be on words that she knew she didn't know, I suggested that a useful strategy is to say "blank" as a placeholder, rather than struggling to pronounce the word.

In my interaction with Sarah during and after her retelling, I touched on the major themes that I believe will help her grow in the future. The most important was quantity of reading of easy and interesting (preferably self-selected) materials. Second was endorsing the value of the strategies she was already using and suggesting some modifications or variations to try out. If I were to work with her over time, I'd see my primary role as helping her to find books she wanted to read and giving her opportunities to talk and perhaps write about them, as well as listening to her read periodically and talking with her about her miscues and strategies. Students who are Sarah's age or older, including adults, are especially well served when we help them develop a strong sense of ownership about their reading and how it works, and an understanding of what they like to read and what strategies they're using.

What's next for Miranda?

When I conducted a miscue analysis with Miranda, it was in the spring of fifth grade, her last year before moving on to middle school. She was definitely able to read independently, but age-appropriate children's literary fiction by writers like Katherine Paterson and Lois Lowry was too hard for her to read on her own; there was definitely a developmental lag compared to other students in her class.

Like Sarah, Miranda needed to do a lot of reading of material that was easy and interesting for her. As far as strategies are concerned, what would be useful for her were more of the kinds of interactions I had with her as she listened to the tape of her reading, focusing on how to use sources of information besides phonics in dealing with unfamiliar words. Also, it would be useful for her to get better at monitoring herself to see if what she was reading made sense. It was also good that she'd come to realize that even good readers make miscues.

Miranda seemed to need more support and teachable-moment interactions than other readers, like Sarah. With Sarah, I could make a suggestion about a strategy to try, and be pretty sure that she'd understood it and could apply it. Miranda needed a lot more hand-holding. But students are who they are: Those who need more teacher support are entitled to it.

Shortly after I'd conducted this miscue analysis with Miranda, I shared it at an inservice presentation with teachers at her school. Since it was a fairly small school with low staff turnover, and Miranda had been identified early as having reading problems, many of the teachers and other staff had worked with her over the years, either in the classroom or in Title I settings.

One of the generalizations about Miranda that I made sure to point out was that she made strong use of phonics in her miscues. One of the teachers commented, "We really are doing okay at teaching phonics here, aren't we?" So often, the knee-jerk reaction to struggling readers (particularly by lay people) is that they just need a good dose of phonics. But Miranda, like many readers having problems, tended to rely on phonics when making miscues *more* than better readers do. The great value of miscue analysis is that it requires us to look at the *whole* picture of the reader, rather than looking at single aspects of the process in isolation.

The power of common sense: Readers show us what they need from us

I hope that in reading these three case examples of how we decide where to go next with a particular reader, you noticed that I was operating not out of any formula or standard prescription but out of paying attention to what the reader was doing. Of course, the more I interacted with a reader, the more sense I had of what she was doing and what the next step for her would be. So much of it really is common sense, isn't it? To become a better reader, you need to read a lot. To be a more effective reader, you need a good variety of strategies. If you feel you're not a good reader, you may need someone to point out your strengths to you. Teachers have important work to do here.

I was aware that in my relatively brief conversation with Sarah, I brought up two simple ideas that seemed to be relatively new to her: the value of reading a lot of material that's easy for you, and the idea of saying "blank" when you know a word is unfamiliar to you. I don't know what her instruction had been like in the twelve years since kindergarten, but what a shame that she would have reached the age of seventeen, in an affluent school district and with the extra time given to special education students, without such basic knowledge about the reading process. Perhaps in the complex world of formal diagnosis and classification and the resultant Individualized Education Plans, we lose sight of what a particular reader is doing well and where he could be helped to improve. So let's next think about some general principles that can guide us in working with students for whom reading is challenging.

What to look for

I'd like to suggest that there are five potentially problematic aspects of the reading process that miscue analysis (including retelling) alerts us to, and that there are very commonsense ways of working with the readers involved. These are: a developmental lag; overuse of phonics; underuse of phonics; problems with comprehension; and self-doubt or self-deprecation as a reader.

Developmental lag

Many struggling readers have adequate to excellent reading strategies, but just aren't reading as well as other students their age. The *Goosebumps* books that the other fourth-graders are reading are just too hard for them. When they hit high school and are expected to read lengthy novels or history textbooks, they may feel overwhelmed. We can metaphorically view such a reader's relationship to a particular text like this; the text is over the reader's head, too hard for her:

TEXT

READER

In the traditional three-reading-group model, the weakest readers in a class are most likely to be asked to read material that's too hard for them; if a "low" reading group in third grade is using a second-grade basal reader, there are bound to be children who are only capable of reading a first-grade book independently. Thus reading in school will always be too hard for them.

When a text is too hard for a reader, there are three ways to bridge the gap:

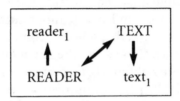

We can provide a link between the reader and the text, as represented by the diagonal line. This approach includes a wide variety of time-honored techniques such as study guides, reading buddies, tutoring and coaching, learning the material in some way other than reading, and so on. When it's necessary for a reader to know the specific content of a particular text, these techniques can be useful, although often time-consuming.

When teachers are provided with textbooks that many of their students can't read, they may avoid the text rather than create links to it, by covering the curriculum material through in-class oral presentations and discussions, particularly in elementary schools. This serves an important goal in providing all students with access to knowledge, but with the disadvantage that students aren't learning through reading. In working with student teachers who plan and teach two lengthy curriculum units as part of their licensing requirements in Oregon, I'm often struck by how little student reading might take place in what are often quite intellectually sophisticated learning experiences.

There are, however, two other ways to bridge the gap between reader and text. We can bring the text down to the reader's level, shown in the figure as $text_1$. In practice, what this means is not doing a complete rewrite of a particular book but providing easier material that covers substantially the same content. For instance, in studying mammals, a teacher might use a science textbook as a resource for deciding on basic concepts that all the students should learn, but then assemble a large collection of trade books with different focuses, formats, and difficulty levels. Then all students can not only learn central ideas and principles about mammals but also learn about mammals through reading.

The third way to bridge reader and text is the most long-term and also the most important; it involves strengthening the reader, thus bringing her up to the level of more difficult texts, as represented in the figure by *reader₁*. If we think about students whose reading just isn't as strong or advanced as that of other students their age, we have a responsibility not only to make accommodations (so that they can continue both to learn and to learn through reading along with their peers) but to help them become better readers.

This may seem like a monumental task, but when a reader's strategies and attitudes are strong, the solution is likely very simple: Read. Period. (Using self-selected material that's easy enough.) Krashen (1993) has assembled a mountain of evidence of, as his book title puts it, the power of reading. An abundance, a multitude, a plenitude of reading is the way we become better readers. If there are concerns about this reader other than just a developmental lag, quantity of reading may not be the entire solution, but it's always a central piece. The teacher's role is twofold: to help students find appropriate things to read, and to avoid insisting that students read material that's too hard, with little or no assistance. Third-graders whose entire reading program involves pushing them through the too-hard second-grade basal reader are being cheated on both counts: too much hard reading and not enough easy reading.

Overuse or underuse of phonics

Phonics (that is, relationships between letters and sounds) is an important part of what readers of an alphabetic language use. To some extent, individual words may map directly on to meaning when we're reading fluently and know the words. This is why we're taken aback when words are replaced with their homophones. An example I just came across is, "Eye trussed their are know miss steaks hear, four my come pewter is all weighs write" (O'Connor, 1999, p. 127).

However, people do often use phonics when we're trying to figure out an unfamiliar word, good readers and weaker readers both. However, good readers also have miscues that don't resemble the text at all, since they're reading efficiently enough that their prediction may in small ways diverge from the print. Weaker readers often seem to go directly (and only) to phonics when stuck, without the range of strategies that good readers have in using phonics in conjunction with the other cueing systems. Readers who overuse phonics need to realize that it's important to come up with something that sounds like a real word and that makes sense, and that if you can't do this, it may be best to say "blank" as a placeholder and move on.

Remember, also, that younger and weaker readers are less able to use phonics than are literate adults. This isn't because of not knowing the rules but because of less experience with reading. An adult, coming across the words *lycanthropy* or *cryptorchidism*, is likely to come up with either the correct pronunciation or one that's very close (look them up to see how you did). It's not because you've consciously applied rules, let alone sounded out letter by letter; rather, you see analogies to other words like *cryptic* and *orchid* and apply them instinctively.

Since phonics instruction has been such a widespread approach to working with struggling readers, it's common to see such readers overuse phonics, as we saw with Sarah and to a greater extent Miranda. The answer is, as we've seen, to help them develop a wider range of strategies. Although there are many books that provide ideas for strategy instruction (see especially Goodman, Watson, & Burke, 1996), a commonsense approach is to observe what the reader's doing and think about a reasonable next step: suggesting that the reader try saying "blank" if she's pretty sure a word isn't one she knows, or see if reading ahead helps the hard words fall into place or reveals that they aren't important to the text as a whole. Readers also need to be able to figure out when a book is just too darn hard for them, with too many unfamiliar words or complex sentence structures.

Sometimes readers will under-attend to the visual cueing system. An example is the young child who appears to be reading a text he's heard a few times but is actually producing a rendition that's a mixture of the text he's heard and a retelling based perhaps on the pictures. A reader who skims too quickly over the surface of the text may be involved not so much in a smooth predictive process as a narration that's only loosely tied to the print on the page. Such readers, of course, need to be helped to attend more closely to the print, through such techniques as guided and assisted reading (Fountas & Pinnell, 1996).

Comprehension problems

If a reader's miscue profile shows some areas of weakness, their understanding of what they've read may well be less than ideal (although they often surprise us in this regard), but there are also students whose oral reading is fine, yet they don't seem to remember or understand what they've read, even with a good deal of probing from the teacher. There are, of course, whole books written on reading comprehension (see especially Goodman, Watson, & Burke, 1997, and Keene & Zimmerman, 1997); however, here I'd like to just mention a few points to help you ensure that you know what's really going on. There are at least five cases where a student's retelling after a miscue analysis may seem weak, but with no real underlying comprehension problem:

1. After a brief retelling, the teacher hasn't done enough probing to draw out details of the reader's understanding.

2. The teacher may have unrealistic expectations about what students should remember of what they've read. After working with a number of students over time, you come to realize that even good readers don't necessarily give highly elaborate summaries.

3. The performance aspect of the oral reading has distracted the reader from a focus on understanding.

4. If a reader can talk knowledgeably about something that's been read to her but not if she reads it herself, the problem may lie not in her comprehension ability but in the relative difficulty of the text for her. If you're having a hard time just reading a text, your attention is distracted from its meaning.

5. The material is on a topic that the reader doesn't know or understand (particularly if it's nonfiction), isn't interested in, or both.

So don't be too quick to jump to a conclusion that a particular reader "just doesn't comprehend"; we get through life by understanding the world around us, and readers who may not appear to grasp what they've read may do just fine when talking about material they enjoy and have chosen themselves.

In general, however, if a student's understanding of what she's read isn't as good as you'd hope, a variety of opportunities to think further about what she's read will be useful. Conferences with you, book discussions with peers, reading books based on movies she's seen—all of these help students become more engaged in and responsive to their reading.

Emotional aspects of reading problems

Students' ideas and feelings about who they are as readers can be thought of as a milieu that permeates their experiences with reading and becomes visible when we talk with them about who they are as readers. For those who have had problems with reading, as they grow older, after more years of painful and frustrating experiences with reading and the self-judgments that come with them, they may use a variety of defenses and coping strategies: arranging their lives and maybe even giving up their dreams so that they won't have to read much;

disparaging reading or devaluing themselves; being defiant because it's less shameful to be bad than stupid. We've all heard the stories and know these students.

The single most important favor we can offer to struggling readers who doubt and criticize themselves (that is to say, the vast majority of them) is to remind them, and ourselves, of the strengths that they do have. You may have noticed, in my profiles of Darcy, Sarah, and Miranda, that positive comments far outnumbered negative ones. We often focus so much on what students can't do, what they don't know, what's wrong with them. Yet everyone is where they are and who they are, and the job of schools is to take all comers. If we're truly able to appreciate that—to accept students as they are, to focus on what's good about what a reader is doing while taking note of what the next area for growth might be—we not only help readers maintain and improve their self-respect and dignity, we give ourselves the chance to see them as clearly as possible, so that we can then work with them effectively.

There are, of course, readers who are so insecure about their abilities that working with them is slow and arduous, punctuated perhaps by many moments of defiance or lethargy. It can take time for a student to build trust both in a teacher and in his own abilities. But this is what we're here for, isn't it?

What about the kids with major problems?

As a contrast to the three readers we've focused on in detail, I'd like to share some miscues from a powerful research study by Peter Board (1982). In this dissertation study, Board was interested in looking at how strong readers and weaker readers fared in different kinds of beginning reading programs. He looked at students from two first-grade classrooms; one of them used a standard basal reader with a sight-word core, while the other used Distar®, a highly structured and scripted phonics-based program. The good readers from each classroom were similar; they used a variety of integrated strategies, their miscues tended to be high-level or self-corrected, and so on. You couldn't tell from their reading which classroom they'd been in.

The reading of the two less proficient readers that Board looked at, however, looked very different from each other, and both looked bizarre. Here's an excerpt from the reading of the student from the basal reader classroom.

The Distar® student's miscues looked like this:

Meel aamduh aaa fegg raass avverree duhaaee
My lamb ate grass every day.

Most teachers, listening to these students read, would be shocked at how poorly they read and perhaps assume that these readers had serious learning disabilities or perhaps even neurological problems. However, the brilliance of Board's study was to look for connections to instruction. He transcribed a number of interactions from each classroom and saw connections between strategies the teachers were modeling and the miscues of these ineffective readers.

In a lesson where a textbook illustration had a picture of a sign saying "Friday is Pet Day," the following exchange occurred:

Teacher: Who can read that sentence? Sheila?

Student #1: Today is—Fish is—

Teacher: It's a day of the week that starts like "fish."
(Board, 1984, p. xx)

Frequently, this teacher prompted students to guess based on the initial letter of a word. And when we look back at the miscues of the weak reader from that classroom, we see that when he came to an unfamiliar word, he guessed based on the first letter (or just skipped it).

The Distar® teacher's instruction was very different. In one typical example, she was working from a chart containing the sentence "The lock is on a rock." It was, as is the case with some of the Distar® materials, written with special symbols and diacritic markings to bring out sound-letter relationships. The interaction, whose form was scripted by the program, was on one occasion as follows:

Teacher: (points to *th* of *the*)

Student: th-th-th

Teacher: (points to *e* of *the*)

Student: eeeee

Teacher: (underlines *the*)

Student: thee

Teacher: (points to *l* of *lock*)

Student: Uhlll-

Teacher: (points to *o* of *lock*)

Student: -aw-aw-aw-

Teacher: (points to *ck* of *lock*)

Student: -awck

Teacher: (underlines *lock*)

Student: lock

This was exactly the kind of procedure that the unsuccessful reader from this classroom was following as he struggled to make sense of text.

Board's explanation of what he discovered posited the concept of an "instruction-dependent personality." The good readers in both classrooms used a variety of strategies that went way beyond what their instruction focused on; reading, for them, was thus an integrated, many-faceted process. The weaker readers did what they'd been taught to do, and only that, and were seriously disabled as a result.

What's the lesson in all of this? When faced with readers with severe problems, there's a tendency to look for answers in the individual, in the brain, in a deficit. However, when a reader has very serious problems, we need to look both more closely and more broadly. We need to spend time listening to her read and talking with her about reading; we need to see what kind of instruction she's had and what she's been reading. There will always be students for whom reading is much more difficult, since people vary. However, we do them a disservice if we're too quick to assume that the problem is inside them, rather than the result of a complex interaction between the learner's abilities, dreams, interests, and feelings; the texts he's exposed to; and the many social environments where learning to read takes place.

11

Miscue Analysis in the Life of the Classroom

Now that you've learned how to conduct a miscue analysis and what to do with it, I'd like to end this book with a vision of how miscue analysis and the knowledge that it reflects might fit into the daily life of your classroom. In writing this, I have the regular classroom teacher in mind, particularly elementary school teachers, but much of it is adaptable to special education and resource room settings, or for work with individuals in a tutoring situation.

I'd like to suggest a variety of ways that miscue analysis is relevant to working with readers beyond its specific role as a diagnostic tool. I'll present these ideas (very) roughly in order of importance.

Developing a miscue ear

It's been said that once you've truly understood miscue analysis, you'll never listen to a reader in the same way again. A focus on understanding what readers are doing and how they're using the cueing systems of written language, as opposed to trying to measure how poorly they're doing and what they're doing wrong, is transformative.

Particularly after you've completed your first miscue analysis, and if you've done so with an awareness of how important your own thinking and understanding are to the process, you'll probably start reacting differently when you hear miscues. When you hear a good student like Darcy read about the morning "computer [rather than *commuter*] traffic," you may well chuckle at how interesting a miscue it is, rather than worry that she needs drill and practice on double consonants. The principles of miscue analysis become a part of your work with students because they're inside your head and have become part of your professional expertise.

Conducting miscue analysis: Who and when?

While you're learning, I'd suggest doing at least three or four miscue analysis sessions, using Procedure III as described in this book, including taping, and a lengthy retelling if possible. It might be interesting for you to conduct one with a good reader, one with an average reader, and one or two with struggling readers, perhaps two very different ones.

After that, I think it's especially valuable to carry out periodic formal miscue analyses with students you're concerned about. It's a very helpful tool for students receiving special services where you need to document where they are as readers and how they're developing as a result of instruction.

There's also a simpler version of miscue analysis, Procedure IV (Goodman, Watson, & Burke, 1987; see Appendix H), which doesn't require tape-recording. As the student reads each sentence, you keep a simple yes-or-no tally of whether each sentence works grammatically and semantically (after the reader has made any corrections), as well as conducting a brief retelling and jotting down some notes. Although it doesn't provide you with as complete a profile as Procedure III does, it's an excellent and relatively simple way to formalize your observations about a reader and compile records about him over time.

Miscue analysis and a readers' workshop classroom

If you're not doing so already, consider making self-selected reading the centerpiece of your classroom reading program. (See Calkins, 2000; Harwayne, 2000; Hindley, 1996 for details of how to do this.) As part of this, regular conferences with students, given your knowledge of how to interpret their miscues, can help you keep tabs on how their reading is going, as well as providing regular opportunities for teachable-moment instruction.

Then every time you have a conference with a student about a book she's reading, jot down a few lines about: (1) her miscues; (2) her understanding of what she read; (3) a good next step for her. Self-adhesive mailing labels, about two-by-three-inches in size, are excellent for this; you can have a sheet or package of them at hand during conferences and then stick them into folders for each student.

Miscues and mini-lessons

When you think about your class as a whole, a sense of student miscues and your concerns about their comprehension can help you plan group

instruction. As students read to you and discuss their reading in conferences, you may become aware, for instance, that many of them get bogged down on proper names, or tangled up in the syntax of long sentences, or don't understand subtleties of character development. One of my tried-and-true rules of thumb for teaching is that when you see a problem, turn it into a mini-lesson, which is a relatively short, focused piece of instruction.

Here's an example. Let's say you notice students having trouble with sentence structures like:

[Darcy's reading] I got to know a lot of people in as close a

1. as
2. in a cl-
3. as a close

relationship as could be achieved in about four seconds. OR

[Miranda's reading] Now, as in thousands of springs pasta

the & thunsed   the

long line of caribou form on the horizon.

from

I might begin by putting a sentence or two like these (preferably sentences that your students have actually had difficulty with) up on an overhead and asking students to read them aloud to a partner. Then ask if the sentences seem sort of hard to them. We could then brainstorm about what to do when you come across a sentence like this and realize that you're having trouble with it, or when you make a miscue that you have a hard time correcting, or when you read a sentence okay but don't really understand it.

There isn't any simple formula for negotiating a complex sentence, but we can brainstorm with students about some possibilities. Maybe a reader can mentally break the sentence down into phrases, or pick out a part that can stand alone (i.e., the main clause) and try to figure out how it relates to the rest of the sentence. Maybe even if a reader isn't sure how all the parts of the sentence fit together, he can still come up with a paraphrase that's adequate even if not perfect. Probably the main idea that you'd want to help students understand is that if you get snarled up in a sentence, it doesn't hurt to take a minute to try to make at least some sense out of it, but not to obsess about it. They can then try this out in their reading over the next couple of days and report back.

Mini-lessons growing out of miscues, then, can serve as ways for students to think actively, with your guidance, about their strategies as readers. You can easily come up with your own ideas based on the

miscues you hear (perhaps one mini-lesson a week?), and you can also turn to a resource book like *Reading Strategies: Focus on Comprehension* (Goodman, Watson, & Burke, 1996).

Reading Detective Club

I'd like to recommend Debra Goodman's excellent book, *The Reading Detective Club* (1999). During her many years of teaching upper elementary grades, Goodman developed a series of experiences to help students develop the same kinds of understanding of miscues that good teachers have. She provides not only a framework for helping students think about how text works and their own reading strategies but a lively series of activities for exploring different aspects of the reading process. For instance, "The Case of the Great Mistake" encourages students to notice mistakes in books and to understand why everyone makes miscues. The first part of the book is an introduction for teachers, but the bulk of it is a reproducible "non-workbook" for kids.

A potpourri of other ideas

1. Have your students use their miscues to decide if a book is easy, hard, or just right for them. They can read a page or two and decide whether or not most of the sentences make sense to them after they've read them.

2. Is your school district considering a new basal reader series or science textbook? Get a sample for your grade level and conduct a miscue analysis with one of your average students and a weaker reader as well. This can provide valuable information for your school about whether they're about to spend a lot of money on books that aren't appropriate for your students.

3. Do a presentation for parents about miscue analysis. Put up overheads of the miscues of good readers, to show parents that mistakes aren't necessarily bad. Then display some miscues of weaker readers and talk about how parents can help them.

4. Use the perspective of miscue analysis to help you be an advocate for the kinds of curriculum you believe in. Write letters to the editor, op-ed pieces, and articles for local education newsletters and journals, celebrating what learners do and the importance of helping them become self-aware about reading strategies rather than being processed through endless workbooks.

5. Learn more! Good starting points are the bibliography and "miscue trilogy" listed here:

Brown, Joel, Goodman, Kenneth S., & Marek, Ann (Eds.). (1996). *Studies in miscue analysis: An annotated bibliography.* Newark, DE: International Reading Association.

Goodman, Yetta M., & Marek, Ann M. (1996). *Retrospective Miscue Analysis: Revaluing readers and reading.* Katonah, NY: Richard C. Owen.

Goodman, Yetta M., Watson, Dorothy J., & Burke, Carolyn L. (1987.) *Reading miscue inventory: Alternative procedures.* Katonah, New York: Richard C. Owen.

Goodman, Yetta M., Watson, Dorothy J., & Burke, Carolyn L. (1996). *Reading strategies: Focus on comprehension* (2nd ed.) Katonah, NY: Richard C. Owen.

Seek out other teachers who have learned how to do miscue analysis, and compare notes about students and miscues.

6. Send me e-mail! If you have questions about miscue analysis or just want to send me a good miscue, I can be reached at wildes@pdx.edu. I don't always have time for lengthy replies, but I will try to respond to every e-mail.

A final note

I've known about miscue analysis for twenty-five years or so now, and I'm still delighted and astonished every time I listen to a student read and every time I analyze miscues. The human mind's drive to create meaning is powerful and thrilling, and miscue analysis gives us a ringside seat. Because of what I know about how reading works, my spontaneous responses even to readers who are struggling quite a bit are always both positive and full of respect for how hard they try and what they're able to accomplish. Through miscue analysis, we can accomplish our vocation as teachers through strengthening what readers can do, but always by beginning with an appreciation and celebration of what they're doing already. I hope that I've been able to share some of this joy and enthusiasm with you, and that you'll explore the power of miscue analysis to help you grow in your knowledge about readers, just by paying close, informed attention to what they do.

Appendix A:
Burke Reading Interview

READING INTERVIEW

Name _____ Age _____ Date _____

Occupation _____ Education Level _____

Sex _____ Interview Setting _____

1. When you are reading and come to something you don't know, what do
    you do?

    Do you ever do anything else?

2. Who is a good reader you know?

3. What makes _____ a good reader?

4.   Do you think _____ ever comes to something she/he doesn't know?

     _____ Yes   _____ No

5.   (Yes) When _____ does come to something she/he doesn't know, what do you think he/she does?

     (No) Suppose _____ comes to something she/he doesn't know. What do you think she/he would do?

6.   If you knew someone was having trouble reading, how would you help that person?

7.   What would a/your teacher do to help that person?

8.   How did you learn to read?

9.   What would you like to do better as a reader?

10. Do you think you are a good reader? Why?

Appendix B:
A Sweet Trip on the Merritt, by Fred Kimmerly

One summer I worked at a toll booth on the Merritt Parkway. I gave out M&M's with the change. It all started when I was looking for a summer job at a youth employment agency in my hometown. They told me that the Greenwich toll station on the Merritt Parkway needed employees for the summer. The job sounded so unusual that I decided to take it.

It was the best job I ever had. I brought a radio to work every day and listened to my favorite station, WBAI. The other toll collectors were some of the nicest and most interesting people that I've ever met. In the morning we would work for an hour or so and then get a half-hour break. On breaks we usually went in the back room of the building at the side of the road. We had a television, a refrigerator, and a stove there.

It was a 20-cent toll. Usually people would give me a quarter and I'd give them a nickel change. One time I was eating some M&M's and accidentally gave one to a driver with his change. Then I thought about doing it for real. At first I only gave them to a few people. I would buy one or two 10-cent packs a day. I steadily gained courage. Before I knew it I was spending $1.50 on M&M's each day. The candy machine kept running out, so I went to a department store and spent money on the big bags. I was now using two pounds a day.

I got to know a lot of people in as close a relationship as could be achieved in about four seconds. Most of them were definitely surprised when they were confronted with something this strange. They could not help but express how they felt. Most of the people liked it. They would laugh and say thank you and maybe eat one or two M&M's that I gave them. Some people threw them on the ground. Many people didn't notice until after they'd pulled out. They might beep, yell, or wave as they drove away (and I'd wave back). People also thought the

M&M's were LSD and that I was a Merry Prankster incognito. A great many people just took their change and shoved it in their pockets. Many of them would never know how M&M's got there. I met one lady who said that it was especially funny to her because she was a behavioral psychologist and used M&M's in working with kids every day.

The best part of the job was the children. Many of them had almost given up waving to people by the time they drove into my booth. Then I'd wave frantically and make faces at them. When their parents put them in charge of giving me the money, they would always enjoy the M&M's.

Soon I acquired a whole constituency of regular customers. I had a different relationship with each person. I would carry on conversations with some people in two-sentence installments. A few people started giving me presents back, like butterscotch jawbreakers and packs of Life Savers. It got so people would drive up and ask for their M&M's. One time I got a chauffeur driving someone to work. About an hour later, a friend of mine who was working on the other side told me that some chauffeur had given him an M&M with his money. Other toll collectors seemed to be wondering why I was having conversations with almost everyone and why people were leaving my booth beeping horns, yelling, and waving; and why I liked to eat so many M&M's.

Things were going fine until I experienced my only major setback. On Hiroshima Day during the morning commuter traffic, I was merrily doing my job until a prosperous-looking executive went through my booth and jammed on his brakes. He opened his door and came up to me and held up a red M&M. I suspected that he thought it was LSD. He asked, "What is this?" "An M&M," I replied. He asked, "What's in it?" To which I replied, "Chocolate, food, you eat it, it's a present." After a short pause he asked, "Are you authorized to give these out?" He finally went into the main building and started yelling at my supervisor about what had happened and telling him to fire me. He was complaining about my giving out dope. My supervisor came out and asked what I'd done. I told them that I had decided to give out an M&M with the change and that this was what had happened. He asked why I'd done such a thing. I said I thought it might be a good joke. He told me that public servants didn't joke around. He made me apologize to the man and left it at that.

I started giving out M&M's again later that day. I was cautious at first. Soon I was back up to two pounds a day, but I never felt secure about executives after that.

About a month later I quit and went on a short camping vacation in Vermont before going away to school. During this vacation I stayed at Goddard College a few days. Out of nowhere this girl came up to me and said, "Hey, I know you from somewhere." I answered, "Well, I worked at a toll booth on the Merritt Parkway this summer." Then she remembered, "that's right! That's right! You gave out M&M's."

In late October of that year I was hitchhiking up to Vermont and got a ride from a person that I'd hit with M&M's at the toll booth. I also heard from the father of a friend that executives in New York City talked of some "joker" on the Merritt Parkway giving out M&M's with the change. I've even picked up hitchhikers who had gone through my booth.

I estimate that I hit about 25,000 people by the time I quit. I think it may have been the most effective and enjoyable political or social thing that I've ever done.

Appendix C: Darcy's Retelling

(Minor interchanges, hesitations, and so on have been edited out.)

Sandra: Great! What did you think of the story?

Darcy: It was good.

Sandra: Do you want to just kind of tell back to me in your own words what it was about, what happened in it, just what you remember about the story?

Darcy: I can't really, you know, explain it all that well.

Sandra: What about the people in it; do you want to start with that? Just tell me who was in the story.

Darcy: A kid who worked—or maybe an older person—who worked in a toll booth giving out, and also gave out M&M's, for change.

Sandra: Were there other people in the story too?

Darcy: Yeah.

Sandra: Who were they?

Darcy: The people who went through the toll booth, and his supervisor.

Sandra: How did the other people react to the M&M's, the people that went through the toll booth, what did they think about the M&M's?

Darcy: Well, they thought different things, like some . . . liked it, and some thought he was giving out dope and one guy got really mad.

Sandra: What happened when the guy got mad?

Darcy: He went to the supervisor and the supervisor told him to stop. No, he didn't tell him to stop giving them out, did he?

Sandra: What did he say, do you remember?

Darcy: No.

Sandra: Did he stop giving them out after that?

Darcy: No.

Sandra: How did he get started in the job, do you remember? How did he start working there?

Darcy: He was looking for a summer job, wasn't he?

Sandra: And why did he happen to pick that job?

Darcy: 'Cause it sounded interesting.

Sandra: Okay, and how did he get started giving out the M&M's?

Darcy: Wasn't it, by mistake one time he gave one out?

Sandra: Then what happened after that?

Darcy: I think, after that he just gave them to a few people and then he got sort of *braver* and decided to give them to everyone who went through.

Sandra: Did all the people eat them right away when they got them?

Darcy: No.

Sandra: What did some do?

Darcy: Some just put them in their pocket with their change. Some threw them out.

Sandra: Did the story end when he quit the job, or did things happen in the story even after he was done with the job?

Darcy: I can't remember that part.

Sandra: Like, did he talk . . .

Darcy: No, he didn't.

Sandra: Okay.

Darcy: Now I know it!

Sandra: Like, did he talk about things, just things that happened while he was there, or things that . . .

Darcy: Well, he talked about the summer—his vacation—and people that he met, and that he'd, something about he'd hit about 25,000 people with them.

Sandra: What did he mean when he said he hit. . . ?

Darcy: Well, he gave them . . .

Sandra: [It] doesn't mean that he threw it at them?

Darcy: No. [laughs] Hope not!

Sandra: Yeah. [laughs] What did he, what happened with some of the people he met afterwards?

Darcy:	When he like . . .
Sandra:	The people that he met, you know, places other than when he was working.
Darcy:	Well, they knew him. One's father had said something about him.
Sandra:	Were there only grownups in the story, or . . . ?
Darcy:	No, there were those kids in the cars, sort of.
Sandra:	What would the kids do?
Darcy:	Wave back at him, and they also gave him the money for the toll booth.
Sandra:	What kind of person do you think that he was, like how would you describe him?
Darcy:	He—I think he's, sort of, what-do-you-call-it, sort of friendly.
Sandra:	Uh huh.
Darcy:	Sort of nutty!
Sandra:	Yeah. [laughs]
Darcy:	*I* wouldn't do that.
Sandra:	Yeah. [laughs] And it would get kind of expensive after a while, wouldn't it? How old do you think he was, about?
Darcy:	Around the age for college.
Sandra:	Did he like his job working at the toll booth?
Darcy:	Yeah.
Sandra:	Why do you think he liked it? What did he like about it?
Darcy:	I don't know. He just seemed to like it, in the story.
Sandra:	Uh huh. Yeah, I guess he met, maybe more than he would've otherwise. Do you . . .
Darcy:	25,000.
Sandra:	Yeah, right. Do you think he learned anything from this job that summer?
Darcy:	Sort of. I think so.
Sandra:	Uh huh. What do you think he learned?
Darcy:	Something about people, sort of. Their attitudes and that.
Sandra:	Uh huh. What about their attitudes?
Darcy:	Well, sort of about what they're like when you give them something and you don't really know them. When, what they think you, they are . . .

Sandra: Uh huh. What are they like when you give them something, like . . . ?

Darcy: Well, some think there's LSD or something and throw them away, and some are friendly, and some don't even know about them.

Sandra: Yeah. So if you had to sum it up in one line what he learned from it, what would you say, what he learned about people?

Darcy: I don't know. There's a lot of friendly people. Because I think most of the ones that he met were friendly. They seemed to be.

Appendix D:
Sample Retelling Form

Text Features	Text Information		Inferences beyond the text; other comments
Characters-who			
Characters-development			
Story line			
Underlying Plot			
Inferences about themes, etc.			
Other comments and impressions			

Form adapted from Board, 1976.

Appendix E: Darcy's Miscues

A Sweet Trip on the Merritt
by Fred Kimmerly

101 One summer I worked at a toll booth

102 on the Merritt Parkway. I gave out

103 M&M's with the change. ~~It~~ ⓒ all started

104 when I was looking ⓒ *at* for a summer job

105 at a youth employment agency *by* in my

106 hometown. They told me that the

107 Ⓥⓒ → Greenwich toll station on the Merritt   1. Gr-ˇ

108 ⓒ *W-* Parkway needed employees for the sum-   2. Gren-
                                                     3. Greenwitch

109 mer. The job sounded so unusual that I   4. Grenwitch

110 decided to take it.

111   It was the best job I ever had. ⓒ I

112 *brought* ~~bought~~ a radio to work every day and

113 listened to my favorite station, WBAI.

114 The other toll collectors were some of

115 the nicest and *the* ^ most interesting people

116 *I* that I've ever met. In the morning we

117 would work for an hour or so and then

118 get a half-hour break. On breaks we usu-

119 ally went in the back room of the build-

120 ing at the side of the road. We had a

121 television, a refrigerator, and a stove

122 there.

123 It was a 20-cent toll. Usually people

124 would give me a quarter and I'd give

125 them a nickel change. One time I was

201 eating some M&M's and accidentally gave one to a driver

202 with his change. Then I thought about doing it for real.

203 At first I only gave them to a few people. I would buy one

204 or two 10-cent packs a day. I steadily gained courage.

205 Before I knew it I was spending $1.50 on M&M's each

206 day. The candy machine kept running out, so I went to a

207 department store and spent money on the big bags. I was

208 now using two pounds a day.

209 I got to know a lot of people in as close a relationship

210 as could be achieved in about four seconds. Most of them

211 were definitely surprised when they were confronted with

212 something this strange. They could not help but express

213 how they felt. Most of the people liked it. They would

214 laugh and say thank you and maybe eat the one or two

215 M&M's that I gave them. Some people threw them on the

216 ground. Many people wouldn't notice until after they'd

217 pulled out. They might beep, ^*or* yell, or wave as they drove

218 away (and I'd wave back). People also thought that the

219 M&M's were LSD Ⓒ and (that) I was a Merry Prankster Ⓡ in-

220 cognito. A great many people just took their change and

221 shoved it in their pockets. Many of them would never

222 know how M&M's got there. I met one lady who said Ⓒ *ma-*

223 that it was especially funny to her because she was a be-

224 havioral psychologist and used M&M's in *work*ing with kids every day. *everyday*

225   The best part of my job was the children. Many of them

226 had almost given up waving to people by the time they

227 drove into my booth. Then I'd wave frantically and make

228 faces at them. When their parents put them in charge of

229 giving me the money, they would always enjoy the M&M's.

230   Soon I acquired a whole constituency of regular cus- *$constistuency*

231 tomers. I had Ⓡ a different relationship with each person. I

232 would carry on conversations with some people in two-

233 sentence installments. A few people started giving me

301 presents back, like butterscotch jawbreakers and packs of

302 Life Savers. It got so that people would drive up Ⓒ *by* and ask

303 for their M&M's. It got to be a problem, however, when

304 they asked ^*their* other toll collectors for their M&M's. One time

305 I got a chauffeur driving someone to work. About an *one* hour

306 later, a friend of mine who was working on the other side

307   told me that some chauffeur had given him an M&M

308   with his money. Other toll collectors seemed to be won-

309   dering why I was having **(C) convershas-** conversations with almost every-

310   one and why people were leaving my booth beeping horns,

311   **(C) w-** yelling, and waving; and why I liked to eat so many M&M's.

312   Things were going fine until I experienced my only

313   major setback. On Hiroshima Day during the morning

314   commuter **computer** traffic, I was merrily doing my job until a pros- **(UC) $ prosperious**

315   perous-looking **(C) ak-** executive went through my booth and

316   jammed (on) his brakes. He opened **(C) the** his door (and) came up

317   to me and held up a red M&M. I suspected that he **$ M-S-P**

318   thought it was LSD. He asked, "What is this?" "An **~What's**

401   M&M," I replied. He asked, "What's in it? To which

402   I replied, "Chocolate, food, you eat (it) it's a present."

403   After a short pause he asked, "Are you authorized to give **said**

404   these out?" He finally went into the main building and

405   started yelling at my supervisor about what had happened and

406   telling him to fire me. He was complaining about

407   my giving out dope. My supervisor came out and asked **(C) me**

408   what I'd done. I told him that I had decided to give out **I'd**

409   an M&M with the change and (that) this was what had **why that**

410   happened. He asked why I'd done such a thing. I said (I)

411   (thought) it might be a good joke. He told me that public **the**

412 servants didn't joke around. He made me apologize to the

413 man and left it at that.

414   I started giving out M&M's again later that day. I was

415 cautious at first. Soon I was back up to two pounds a day,

416 but I never felt secure about executives after that.

417   About a month later I quit and went on a short camping

418 vacation in Vermont before going away to school. During

419 this vacation I stayed at Goddard College a few days. Out

420 of nowhere this girl came up to me and said, "Hey, I

421 know you from somewhere." I answered, "Well, I worked

422 at a toll booth on the Merritt Parkway this summer." Then

423 she remembered, "that's right! That's right! You gave out

424 M&M's."

425   In late October of that year I was hitchhiking up to

426 Vermont and got a ride from a person that I'd hit with

427 M&M's at the toll booth. I also heard from the father of

428 a friend that executives in New York City talked of some

429 "joker" on the Merritt Parkway giving out M&M's with

430 the change. I've even picked up hitchhikers who had gone

431 through my booth.

432   I estimate that I hit about 25,000 people by the time I

433 quit. I think it may have been the most effective and

434 enjoyable political or social thing that I've ever done.

Appendix F:
Darcy's Coded Story

1   One summer I worked at a toll booth on the Merritt   *YYN*

     Parkway.

2   I gave out M&M's with the change.   *YYN*

3   It all started when I was looking for a summer job at a

     youth employment agency in my hometown.   *YYN*

4   They told me that the Greenwich toll station on the   *1. Gr~*   *TYP*
       2. Gren
     Merritt Parkway needed employees for the summer.   *3. Greenwitch*
       4. Grenwitch

5   The job sounded so unusual that I decided to take it.   *YYN*

6   It was the best job I ever had.   *YYN*

7   I brought a radio to work every day and listened to my

     favorite station, WBAI.   *YYN*

8   The other toll collectors were some of the nicest and most

     interesting people that I've ever met.   *YYN*

9   In the morning we would work for an hour or so and then

     get a half-hour break.   *YYN*

10 On breaks we usually went ~~in~~ *out* the back room ~~of~~ *©f-* the build- YYN

ing at the side of the road.

11 We had a television, a refrigerator, and a stove there. YYN

12 *It's* It was a 20-cent toll. YYN

13 Usually people would give me a quarter and I'd give them

a nickel change. YYN

14 One time I was eating some M&M's and *©* *actually* *(H)* accidentally gave

one to a driver with his change. YYN

15 Then I thought about doing it for real. YYN

16 At first I only gave them to a few people. YYN

17 I would buy one or two 10-cent packs a day. YYN

18 I steadily gained courage. YYN

19 Before I knew it I was spending $1.50 on M&M's each day. YYN

20 The candy machine kept running out, so I went to a

department store and spent money on the big bags. YYN

21 I was now using two pounds a day. YYN

22 I got to know a lot of people *©* → in as close a relationship *©* as

I© could be achieved in about four seconds.
1. as
2. in ad-
3. as a close
NN –

23 Most of them were definitely surprised when they were

confronted with something this strange. YYN

24 They could not help but express how they felt. YYN

25 Most *of the* people liked it. YYN

26 They would laugh and say thank you and maybe eat *the*

one or two M&M's that I gave (them) YYN

27   Some people threw them on the ground. YYN

28   Many people ⓒdidn't ⊖ wouldn't notice until after they'd pulled out. YYN

29   They might beep, ^or yell, or wave as they drove away (and I'd

wave back). YYN

30   People also thought that the M&M's were ⓒ(LSD and (that) I

was a Merry Prankster ⓡincognito. YYN

31   A great many people just took their change and shoved it

in their pockets. YYN

32   Many of them would never know how ⓒma- (M&M's) got there. YYN

33   I met one lady who said that it was especially funny to her

because she was a behavioral psychologist and used

M&M's in work ⓗworking with kids every everyday day. YYN

34   The best part of my job was the children. YYN

35   Many of them had almost given up waving to people by

the time they drove into my booth. YYN

36   Then I'd wave frantically and make faces at them. YYN

37   When their parents put them in charge of giving me the

money, they would always enjoy the M&M's. YYN

38   Soon I acquired a whole ₴constistuency ⓗconstituency of regular customers. YN—

39   I had ⓡ a different relationship with each person. YYN

40   I would carry on conversations with some people in two-

sentence installments. YYN

41   A few people started giving me presents back, like butter-

scotch jawbreakers and packs of Life Savers.   YYN

42   It got so that people would drive up and ask for their   YYN

M&M's.

43   It got to be a problem, however, when they asked other toll

collectors for their M&M's.   YYN

44   One time I got a chauffeur driving someone to work.   YYN

45   About an hour later, a friend of mine who was working on

the other side told me that some chauffeur had given him

an M&M with his money.   YYN

46   Other toll collectors seemed to be wondering why I was

having conversations with almost everyone and why peo-

ple were leaving my booth beeping horns, yelling, and wav-

ing; and why I liked to eat so many M&M's.   YYN

47   Things were going fine until I experienced my only major

setback.   YYN

48   On Hiroshima Day during the morning commuter traffic,

I was merrily doing my job until a prosperous-looking

executive went through my booth and jammed on his   YN-

brakes.

49   He opened his door and came up to me and held up a red

M&M.   YN-

50   I suspected that he thought it was LSD.   YYN

51 He asked, "What is this?"   *What's,*   ΥΥN

52 "An M&M," I replied.   ΥΥN

53 He asked, "What's in it?   ΥΥN

54 To which I replied, "Chocolate, food, you eat it, it's a pre-

sent."   ΥΥN

55 After a short pause he asked, "Are you authorized to give   *said ⑤*

these out?"   ΥΥN

56 He finally went into the main building and started yelling

at my supervisor about what had happened and telling

him to fire me.   ΥΥN

57 He was complaining about my giving out dope.   *ⒸmeⒽ*   ΥΥN

58 My supervisor came out and asked what I'd done.   ΥΥN

59 I told him that I had decided to give out an M&M with the   *I'd*

change and that this was what had happened.   *why thatⒽ*   ΥΥN

60 He asked why I'd done such a thing.   ΥΥN

61 I said I thought it might be a good joke.   ΥΥN

62 He told me that public servants didn't joke around.   *the*   *don't Ⓗ*   *here*   ΥΥP

63 He made me apologize to the man and left it at that.   *he*   ΥΥN

64 I started giving out M&M's again later that day.   ΥΥN

65 I was cautious at first.   ΥΥN

66 Soon I was back up to two pounds a day, but I never felt

secure about executives after that.   ΥΥN

67 About a month later I quit and went on a short camping

VERmont (H)

vacation in Vermont before going away to school.   ΥΥΡ

with the Goddards

68 During this vacation I stayed at Goddard College a few   NN−

day (H)
days.

(C) it (N)

69 Out of nowhere this girl came up to me and said, "Hey, I

know you from somewhere."   ΥΥΝ

was working   (C) at (S)

70 I answered, "Well, I worked at a toll booth on the Merritt

Parkway this summer."   ΥΥΝ

71 Then she remembered, "that's right! That's right! You gave

out M&M's."   ΥΥΝ

72 In late October of that year I was hitchhiking up to

VERmont
Vermont and got a ride from a person (that) I'd hit with

in (S)
M&M's at the toll booth.   ΥΥΡ

73 I also heard from the father of a friend that executives in

about (N)
New York City talked of some "joker" on the Merritt

Parkway giving out M&M's with the change.   ΥΥΝ

I'd (H)   who'd
74 I've even picked up hitchhikers who had gone through my

booth.   ΥΥΝ

75 I estimate that I hit about 25,000 people by the time I quit.   ΥΥΝ

76 I think it may have been the most effective and enjoyable

political or social thing that I've ever done.   ΥΥΝ

Appendix G: Coding Sheet

	Question #1 (syntax)		Question #2 (semantics)	
	number	*percent*	*number*	*percent*
Yes, acceptable				
No, not acceptable				
Total		100%		100%

	Question #3 (meaning change)	
	number	*percent*
No meaning change		
Partial meaning change		
Yes, major meaning change		
Total (count only those coded, not dashes)		100%

	Graphic (visual similarity)	
	Number	*Percent*
High		
Some		
None		
Total		100%

Thoughts about the reading:

Thoughts about the retelling:

Appendix H: Procedure IV

Reader _____ Date _____

Teacher _____ Age/Grade _____

Selection _____

Does the sentence, as the reader left it, make sense within the context of the story?

Yes _____ Total _____

No _____ Total _____

Number of Sentences _____ Comprehending Score _____

Divide the total Yes by Total number of sentences for Comprehending Score

_____

Retelling information

_____

Comments

(Goodman, Watson, Burke) © 1987 Richard C. Owen Publishers, Inc.

Appendix I: Checklist

I. Conducting the reading

   A. Pick appropriate reading material.
   B. Make a copy of the text for yourself and get a tape recorder.
   C. Set the reader at ease.
   D. Give directions.
      1. You'll be asking him to discuss the story after reading it.
      2. If he gets stuck, he should do what he'd usually do if there was no one there to help.
   E. Listen to the reading, writing down as many of the miscues as possible.
   F. Conduct the retelling.
      1. Unassisted retelling
      2. Assisted retelling
      3. Probing of miscues and other areas of interest
   G. (Optional) Reader listens and reacts to her own miscues on tape (retrospective miscue analysis).

II. Coding and analyzing the miscues.

   A. Number the sentences. In the margin of the text, or on a separate form, answer the following questions for each sentence, as it reads after all the reader's corrections:
      1. Does it sound like an English sentence? (Is it syntactically acceptable?) Y or N?
      2. Does it make sense? (Is it semantically acceptable?) Y or N? (If question #1 was answered N, Question #2 must be also.)
      3. If Questions #1 and #2 were answered Y, did any miscues change the meaning of the sentence? Y (major change), P (partial change), or N (no change)? If Questions #1 and #2 were not both answered Y, put a dash for Question #3.

B. For each miscue where a single word was substituted for another single word, mark it on your copy of the story according to the graphic or visual similarity between the miscue and text: H (high), S (some), or N (none).
C. Tabulate the numbers and percentages on the data sheet.
D. Write some notes about your impressions of the reading and retelling.

References

Adams, Marilyn J. (1990). *Beginning to read: Thinking and learning about print*. Cambridge, MA: MIT Press.

Barrie, J. M. (1911). *Peter Pan* (originally published as *Peter and Wendy*). New York: Scribner's.

Board, Peter. (1976). Retelling form. Unpublished paper. Toronto: University of Toronto.

Board, Peter. (1982). Toward a theory of instructional influence: Aspects of the instructional environment and their influence on children's acquisition of reading (Unpublished doctoral dissertation, University of Toronto).

Bormuth, John R. (1968). The cloze readability procedure. *Elementary English, 55,* 429–436.

Brown, Joel, Goodman, Kenneth S., & Marek, Ann (Eds.). (1996). *Studies in miscue analysis: An annotated bibliography*. Newark, DE: International Reading Association.

Burke, Carolyn. (1987). Reading Interview. In Yetta M. Goodman, Dorothy J. Watson, & Carolyn L. Burke, *Reading miscue inventory: Alternative procedures* (pp. 219–220). New York: Richard C. Owen.

Burnett, Frances H. (1911). *The secret garden*. Retrieved from Project Gutenberg (http://www.promo.net/pg).

Calkins, Lucy M. (2000). *The art of teaching reading*. New York: Addison-Wesley.

Carkeet, David. (1997). *The error of our ways*. New York: Henry Holt.

Clay, Marie. (1979). *The early detection of reading difficulties*. Portsmouth, NH: Heinemann.

Clay, Marie, & Johnston, Peter H. (1992). Recording oral reading: Making sense of records of oral reading. In Peter H. Johnston (Ed.), *Constructive evaluation of literate activity* (pp. 67–94). New York: Longman.

Dawkins, Richard. (1995). *River out of Eden: A Darwinian view of life* (Science Masters Series). New York: Basic Books.

Fountas, Irene C., & Pinnell, Gay Su. (1996). *Guided reading: Good first teaching for all children.* Portsmouth, NH: Heinemann.

Goodman, Debra. (1999). *The reading detective club: Solving the mysteries of reading: A teacher's guide.* Portsmouth, NH: Heinemann.

Goodman, Kenneth S. (1973). Miscues: Windows on the reading process. In Kenneth S. Goodman (Ed.), *Miscue analysis: Applications to reading instruction* (pp. 3–14). Urbana, IL: ERIC and NCTE.

Goodman, Kenneth S. (1976). The Goodman Taxonomy of Reading Miscues. In P. David Allen & Dorothy Watson (Eds.), *Findings of research in miscue analysis: Classroom implications* (pp. 157–244). Urbana, IL: ERIC and NCTE.

Goodman, Kenneth S. (1982). *Language and literacy: The selected writings of Kenneth S. Goodman* (Vol. I: Process, Theory, Research) (Frederick V. Gollasch, Ed.). Boston: Routledge & Kegan Paul.

Goodman, Kenneth S. (1996). A mardsan giberter for Farfie. In Kathryn F. Whitmore & Yetta M. Goodman (Eds.), *Whole language voices in teacher education* (p. 139). York, ME: Stenhouse.

Goodman, Yetta M. (1978). Kid watching: An alternative to testing. *National Elementary Principal, 57,* 41–45.

Goodman, Yetta M., & Marek, Ann M. (1996). *Retrospective miscue analysis: Revaluing readers and reading.* Katonah, NY: Richard C. Owen.

Goodman, Yetta M., Watson, Dorothy J., & Burke, Carolyn L. (1987). *Reading miscue inventory: Alternative procedures.* Katonah, NY: Richard C. Owen.

Goodman, Yetta M., Watson, Dorothy J., & Burke, Carolyn L. (1996). *Reading strategies: Focus on comprehension* (2nd ed.) Katonah, NY: Richard C. Owen.

Harris, Theodore L., & Hodges, Richard E. (Eds.). (1995). *The literary dictionary: The vocabulary of reading and writing.* Newark, DE: International Reading Association.

Harwayne, Shelley. (2000). *Lifetime guarantees: Toward ambitious literacy teaching.* Portsmouth, NH: Heinemann.

Henry, O. (1906). The gift of the Magi. Retrieved from Project Gutenberg (http://www.promo.net/pg).

Hindley, Joanne. (1996). *In the company of children.* Portsmouth, NH: Heinemann.

Huey, Edmond B. (1968). *The psychology and pedagogy of reading.* Cambridge, MA: MIT Press. (Originally published 1918.)

Jackson, Tim. (1997). *Inside Intel: Andrew Grove and the rise of the world's most powerful chip company.* New York: Dutton.

Keene, Ellin O., & Zimmerman, Susan. (1997). *Mosaic of thought: Teaching comprehension in a reader's workshop.* Portsmouth, NH: Heinemann.

Kimmerly, Fred. (1975). A sweet trip on the Merritt. *New York Magazine.*

Kolers, Paul. (1969). Reading is only incidentally visual. In Kenneth S. Goodman & James T. Fleming (Eds.), *Psycholinguistics and the teaching of reading* (pp. 8–16). Newark, DE: International Reading Association.

Krashen, Steven D. (1993). *The power of reading.* Englewood, CO: Libraries Unlimited.

McWhorter, John. (2000). *Spreading the word: Dialect and language in America.* Portsmouth, NH: Heinemann.

Miller, George A. (1977). *Spontaneous apprentices: Children and language.* New York: Seabury.

Miller, George A. (1996). *The science of words.* New York: Scientific American Library.

Moustafa, Margaret. (1997). *Beyond traditional phonics: Research discoveries and reading instruction.* Portsmouth, NH: Heinemann.

O'Connor, Patricia T. (1999). *Words fail me: What everyone who writes should know about writing.* Orlando, FL: Harcourt.

Pandell, Karen. (1993). *Land of dark, land of light: The Arctic National Wildlife Refuge.* New York: Dutton.

Perry, Theresa, & Delpit, Lisa. (1998). *The real Ebonics debate: Power, language, and the education of African-American children.* Boston: Beacon.

Rhodes, Lynn K., & Dudley-Marling, Curt. (1996). *Readers and writers with a difference: A holistic approach to teaching struggling readers and writers* (2nd ed.). Portsmouth, NH: Heinemann.

Ruddell, Robert, Ruddell, Martha R., & Singer, Harry (Eds.). (1994). *Theoretical models and processes of reading* (4th ed.). Newark, DE: International Reading Association.

Scieszka, Jon, & Smith, Lane. (1992). *The stinky cheese man and other fairly stupid tales.* New York: Viking.

Smith, Frank. (1997). *Reading without nonsense* (3rd ed.). New York: Teachers College Press.

Smith, Frank. (1988). *Understanding reading* (4th ed.). Hillsdale, NJ: Erlbaum.

Watson, Dorothy J., & Crowley, Paul. (1988). How can we implement a whole language approach? In Constance Weaver, *Reading process and practice: From socio-psycholinguistics to whole language* (pp. 232–279). Portsmouth, NH: Heinemann.

Weaver, Constance. (1994). Reconceptualizing reading and dyslexia. *Journal of Childhood Communication Disorders, 16,* 23–35.

Wilde, Sandra. (1997). *What's a schwa sound anyway?: A holistic guide to phonetics, phonics, and spelling.* Portsmouth, NH: Heinemann.

Worsnop, Chris. (1980). *A procedure for using the technique of the Reading Miscue Inventory as a remedial teaching tool with adolescents.* Unpublished paper. (ERIC Document Reproduction Service Document ED 324 644.)